# Dark Goddess Spirituality

*Embrace the Transformative Power of
Divine Femininity*

© Copyright 2025 - All rights reserved.

The content contained within this book may not be reproduced, duplicated, or transmitted without direct written permission from the author or the publisher.

Under no circumstances will any blame or legal responsibility be held against the publisher or author for any damages, reparation, or monetary loss due to the information contained within this book, either directly or indirectly.

**Legal Notice:**

This book is copyright-protected. It is only for personal use. You cannot amend, distribute, sell, use, quote, or paraphrase any part of the content within this book without the consent of the author or publisher.

**Disclaimer Notice:**

Please note the information contained within this document is for educational and entertainment purposes only. All effort has been executed to present accurate, up-to-date, reliable, and complete information. No warranties of any kind are declared or implied. Readers acknowledge that the author is not engaging in the rendering of legal, financial, medical, or professional advice. The content within this book has been derived from various sources. Please consult a licensed professional before attempting any techniques outlined in this book.

By reading this document, the reader agrees that under no circumstances is the author responsible for any losses, direct or indirect, that are incurred as a result of the use of the information contained within this document, including, but not limited to, errors, omissions, or inaccuracies.

# Your Free Gift
# (only available for a limited time)

Thanks for getting this book! If you want to learn more about various spirituality topics, then join Mari Silva's community and get a free guided meditation MP3 for awakening your third eye. This guided meditation mp3 is designed to open and strengthen ones third eye so you can experience a higher state of consciousness. Simply visit the link below the image to get started.

https://spiritualityspot.com/meditation

### Or, Scan the QR code!

# Table of Contents

**PART 1: DARK GODDESSES** ............................................................. 1
   INTRODUCTION ............................................................................ 2
   CHAPTER 1: THE ARCHETYPE OF THE DARK GODDESS ....... 4
   CHAPTER 2: GREEK GODDESSES ............................................... 13
   CHAPTER 3: EGYPTIAN GODDESSES ......................................... 24
   CHAPTER 4: MESOPOTAMIAN GODDESSES ............................ 36
   CHAPTER 5: SLAVIC GODDESSES ............................................... 45
   CHAPTER 6: HINDU GODDESSES ............................................... 54
   CHAPTER 7: AFRICAN GODDESSES .......................................... 68
   CHAPTER 8: CELTIC/IRISH GODDESSES .................................. 79
   CHAPTER 9: NORSE GODDESSES ............................................... 91
   CHAPTER 10: EMBRACING THE DARK GODDESS WITHIN ... 102
   CHAPTER 11: HONORING THE DARK GODDESSES: RITUALS AND PRACTICES ......................................................................... 108
   TABLES OF CORRESPONDENCES ........................................... 115
   CONCLUSION ............................................................................ 140
**PART 2: BLACK MADONNA** ......................................................... 142
   INTRODUCTION ........................................................................ 143
   CHAPTER 1: WHO IS THE BLACK MADONNA? ..................... 145
   CHAPTER 2: HER SACRED ARTISTRY .................................... 154
   CHAPTER 3: HER THEMES AND SYMBOLISM ...................... 160
   CHAPTER 4: HER TRANSFORMATIVE POWER ..................... 167
   CHAPTER 5: HER RELATION TO MOTHER GODDESSES ..... 179

CHAPTER 6: ESOTERIC INTERPRETATIONS ................................................ 191
CHAPTER 7: CONNECTING WITH THE BLACK MADONNA ................ 201
CHAPTER 8: HEALING THROUGH THE DIVINE FEMININE ................ 211
CHAPTER 9: HONORING THE MOTHER GODDESS ............................... 220
CONCLUSION ........................................................................................................ 228
APPENDIX: LIST OF BLACK MADONNAS ................................................... 230
HERE'S ANOTHER BOOK BY MARI SILVA THAT YOU MIGHT LIKE .......................................................................................................................... 244
YOUR FREE GIFT (ONLY AVAILABLE FOR A LIMITED TIME) ................ 245
REFERENCES ....................................................................................................... 246
IMAGE SOURCES ................................................................................................ 260

# Part 1: Dark Goddesses

*Unlocking the Power of Hecate, Lilith, The Morrigan, Baba Yaga, Kali, Oya, Persephone, Hathor, Sekhmet, and More*

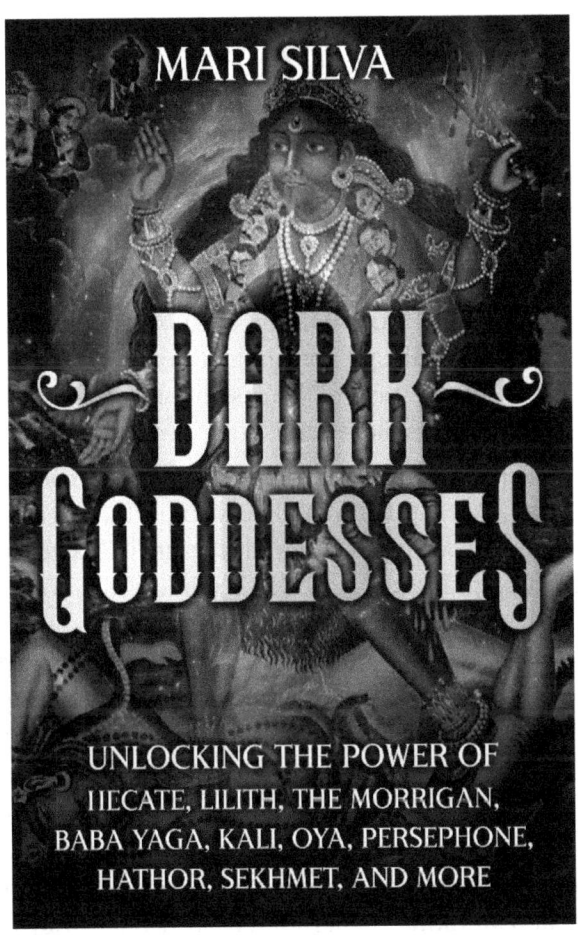

# Introduction

Feared by many and venerated by others, and with their origins, roles, and true powers often shrouded in mystery, the Dark Goddesses are unique representations of negative forces in different cultures. Every culture had them in its pantheon, and, in some, they were even more respected than the benevolent deities because no one dared to anger them. This book explores the archetype of these Dark Goddesses, unveiling what made them so powerful and significant for ancient and modern followers alike. You will learn how they're tied to Jung's theory of the shadow self and how this might lead to the exploration of one's inner Dark Goddess.

This book presents a multilayered insight into the roles and attributes of Greek, Egyptian, Mesopotamian, Slavic, Hindu, African, Celtic, and Norse Dark Goddesses. Unlike other books in its category, which only focus on the mythological aspects of these deities, this book also explores their history and spiritual significance for modern spiritual seekers. Whether you are just dipping your toes into spiritual practices or have some experience in shadow work, goddess worship, neo-paganism, and other alternative practices, this book will empower you to unlock the transformative potential and inner wisdom Dark Goddesses embody.

The book relays theoretical and practical information in a beginner-friendly, easily-to-grasp way, making it easier for everyone to relate to and enrich their spiritual journey. Whether you're open to exploring different spiritual paths and looking to embrace a diverse range of spiritual traditions or wish to learn about the dark deities from a specific culture, this book will be the perfect stepping stone for your new adventures.

If you relate to the divine feminine and are seeking knowledge and inspiration from powerful female deities, this guide will show you how to obtain it all from the right sources. Through a profound and esoteric exploration of the darker sides of the goddesses, this book will teach you how to acknowledge the complexity of their symbolism, myths, and, most importantly, the vast empowerment they can bestow on you. If you are ready to expand your spiritual wisdom through a profound understanding and embracing female divine energies, don't hesitate to read on.

# Chapter 1: The Archetype of the Dark Goddess

To help you understand the origins, symbolism, and meaning of the term "Dark Goddess," this chapter explores the concept of darkness in multifaceted contexts of spirituality, psychology, and mythology in a range of cultures and spiritual traditions. After introducing the book's central theme and the significance of transformation through the darkness and shadow, this chapter outlines a deeper perspective, including primary and esoteric information about the Dark Goddess archetype.

## The Concept of the Dark Goddess

The concept of Dark Goddesses is based on an archetype representing similar roles, attributes, and functions in different cultures. Esoterically speaking, the archetype is defined as a causal presence of a causal energy or one that lives in the causal part of the spirit, known as the *psyche*. It is created (naturally through thoughts or magical acts) in the psyche, and it can die there, too, if its energy ceases to exist. This indicates that the Dark Goddess archetype is a living being that only manifests in people's psyche. Once created, the archetype continues to be present in the causal continuum, meaning it affects people's lives because they believe in it.

These female deities became associated with war and destruction.[1]

As the New Age pagan and other alternative religions gained popularity, the idea of these powerful dark beings grew alongside this renewed interest. The reason behind this was simple. While often misunderstood, Dark Goddesses are the ultimate representation of authenticity and diversity. Working with a Dark Goddess enables you to shine a light on these topics - and many others that are repressed by modern society. Because they may be pushed aside, they remain lurking in the shadows, just like dark female deities do in legends. They can guide the practitioner toward healing, which is often seen as rebirth as it frees them from societal expectations and other burdens that obstruct their authenticity. Due to its prominent energy, the archetype is a true powerhouse, capable of rewriting the narratives of the lives of those seeking freedom and empowerment through the divine feminine.

As an archetype, the Dark Goddess is only one facet of a female deity. Many turn to work with ancient goddesses because they promise brightness and positivity. However, sometimes, life forces you to explore the goddess's other side because they often hold answers to negative experiences, thoughts, and emotions. In fact, the deities identified with this archetype are only called Dark Goddesses because of their controversial portrayal by certain cultures who didn't understand their roles and origins. In cultures where patriarchal views were prevalent, these female deities became associated with war and destruction, with many a patriarch claiming they had an unusual desire to spill blood. By contrast, in cultures that embrace and honor dark female energies, the Dark Goddess is seen as part of a whole, the part that deals with frightening and troublesome yet necessary experiences of life. While the lighter sides nurture, heal, and protect, the darker ones teach how to fight, confront your enemies (both physically and metaphorically), and overcome the most formidable obstacles in life. In many legends and stories, the Dark Goddesses were summoned to chase away true evil and purify the space/person/object it inhabited.

## Jungian Analysis and the Shadow Self

Mysterious, destructive, chaotic, associated with the occult - the Dark Goddess archetype is all that. However, it is also transformational as it provides a holistic insight into oneself and nature. The nature of these female deities is also dark, which, on one hand, is indicative of the female empowerment experience. On the other hand, this nature is the perfect embodiment of what renowned psychologist Carl Jung called the "shadow self."

In multiple religions, the Dark Goddess archetype is the part of nature that should be avoided or prevented from flourishing. Despite differences in their backstories, Dark Goddesses in Eastern and Western cultures were viewed similarly. One of the key differences was that in Western cultures, the archetype was seen as the projection of patriarchy, hence the association with hostile intentions and warfare.

When referring to human nature, darkness was also something people were encouraged to stay away from. While it's easy to see why one would want to discourage people from approaching and embracing one's darkest self, repressing it is also not recommended because it prevents them from understanding their true nature, values, and spiritual needs. Since this is a much-debated topic in religious communities and among alternative practitioners, understanding the archetype's significance for personal empowerment requires a deeper exploration. This is where delving into Jung's psychodynamics and theoretical analysis of the human psyche comes in handy.

While Gustav Jung was primarily concerned about the human psyche, he and his students also thoroughly researched the goddess concept, effectively drawing a line between psychoanalysis and esoteric practices. Jung named the goddess anime, or animal mundi (which translates as world soul), implicating not only that people live in a goddess-centered world but that the goddess lives within everyone.

According to Jung, the Dark Goddess archetype is the manifestation of the "shadow self," standing in opposition to the "ego self." The self represents the entirety of the psyche, combining the subconscious and conscious parts. As the most authentic core of one's being, the self gives way to traits and characters, including the persona and the anima/animus; the latter are gendered parts of the collective subconscious. The anima is how the male psyche envisions the feminine, and the animus is how the female psyche infers the male one. The persona is the part of yourself you convey to the world.

Jung saw the ego as the core and main driver of one's persona - the part everyone is conscious of and controls through their actions. However, Jung considered that there must be a balance to the ego, partially because while treating patients, he discovered that deep down, people are always aware of their true nature and personality even if they don't show this awareness to the outside world. He called this hidden part "the shadow" and argued that reaching it requires immense effort. However, by raising awareness of one's shadow self, you can identify the darkest aspects of your personality and acknowledge them as real parts of your existence. For most people, this goes against their every core belief, so they'll naturally resist conceding to their shadow self. The main reason for resistance can be found in the patriarchal theological concept of evil, which dictates that the dark part of oneself is bad and, therefore, must be repressed.

Jung called the process of raising self-awareness of one's complex nature Individuation. According to him, facing one's shadow is the first step on this journey. Instead of viewing the dark side as something to be ashamed of, Jung encouraged people to confront the part of themselves that prompts them to do evil things. He claimed that since these are natural parts of everyone's personality, it's better to get to know them closely rather than to avoid it as if it would lead to a road of corruption. He considered that seeing the shadow as inherently flawed can do more harm to your psyche than embracing it and trying to work with it.

Jung's theory about the Dark Goddess archetype being the epitome of the shadow self offers a fantastic way to describe and experience internalized experiences. What's ineffable to some people, followers of Dark Goddesses can embrace it as a natural experience without any biases, doubt, or questions. Regardless of what your beliefs are, the goddess teaches you about the importance of experience, effectively validating the things you can't explain through rational thoughts and concepts.

Jung's theories provide an empowering and genuine intrinsic source of power in the Dark Goddess. Whether it was through identifying her as an individual female divinity in a vast pantheon of deities or seeing her as the face of a multi-faceted goddess, this is exactly how the archetype is portrayed in several religions. Buttressing Jung's claims of how much effort it requires to face the darkness within, many tales describe the high price paid by those approaching the goddess. Known to bring people to the edge of extreme psychological exhaustion, these dark female forces demand a great deal. You cannot simply hope for the best when encountering these deities, which is why interaction with them is ill-advised unless you are truly prepared to handle their power.

On more than one occasion, practitioners describe experiencing a significant negative shift when calling on a Dark Goddess. Considering Jung's theories, this is to be expected. After all, confronting one's dark self also brings up many negative emotions, including fear, helplessness, anxiety, and weakness. Yet, without experiencing these, you cannot learn your own strength. If you never face anything that upsets or scares you, how do you know you'll have the courage to overcome it? Only by confronting your weaknesses can you ever understand what it takes to summon your strength. It's a powerful but much-needed lesson the archetype teaches. The goddesses also show that just as everyone can be compassionate and loving when empowered, their power can also come from anger, pain, and other negative emotions and experiences (and use it for great purposes).

While facing your dark self often results in the destruction of previous beliefs, this is necessary to rebuild yourself. Before working with the Dark Goddess, you're only living driven by the conscious part of yourself. Afterward, you become whole and find your individual strength. This is where the true power of the Dark Goddess archetype lies.

Over time, Jung's theories that tied the archetype to a person's personality and psyche became widely accepted. Some were purely intrigued by this mysterious power, while others realized the importance of further exploration of this highly neglected archetype. Interestingly enough, Jung viewed the Dark Goddess both as a female shadow self (anima) and the dark aspect of the male shadow (animus). The latter explains why so many people don't want to concede to this aspect within their psyche. It goes against the male ego, which doesn't like to think it has weaknesses, fears, and insecurities. However, its shadow knows it does, and contrary to other popular beliefs, it's not evil or negative either. The female shadow empowers the person to acknowledge this part of their psyche, weaknesses, faults, and all.

The multitude of Dark Goddesses you can work with have their own particular powers. By summoning the ones you identify with or truly need, you can find the way forward in your empowerment journey. For example, by calling on a goddess symbolizing freedom and lust, you can learn to suppress your guilt about not following societal expectations blindly (virtually no one does because it's impossible given how many there are and how baffling they can be). Likewise, by summoning a goddess of transformation, you can heal from past traumas and use them instead to illustrate growth.

Those following in Jung's footsteps helped transform the goddess from a simple archetype into a full-blown movement. They brought the archetype alive from the causal psyche and into the real world, proving its existence. This helped popularize the concept of the divine feminine, both in its own transcendent nature (which helps identify it in oneself) and as the driving force behind new and re-emerging religions that worship Dark Goddesses as transcendent divine beings.

## Dark Goddess Archetype Representations

In many cultures, the Dark Goddess is seen as a sinister female creature with origins in ancient traditions, much older than the myths of their benevolent counterparts. Known as the Mother of Blood and Mistress of Destruction, among others, this archetype's contemporary definition is often tied to how these female deities are represented in popular religions and traditions. These often illustrate dark female deities as beautiful women in their prime, wearing provocative clothing or even having a naked form. They also claim that in ancient times, these goddesses could only be appeased via human sacrifices and were never to be addressed by their names.

Yet, in the same vein, these representations empower women beyond the ways they are depicted in their benevolent, nurturing goddess form. While it's true that this empowerment comes from the divine female's sinister ability to dabble in the occult, it can't be denied that they play vital roles in people's lives, evolution, and collective growth. Female empowerment may be hidden behind esoteric concepts and mysterious and misunderstood pagan practices, yet it's clear that women can obtain it by working on themselves and developing their ability to control their entire self.

Unlike some pagan and Wiccan practitioners who see the divine feminine as a calm, serene, yet independent ethos, the depiction of the Dark Goddess archetype isn't afraid to highlight the dark feminine principle. Women don't have to adopt a male behavior to be as powerful as men are. They can find the empowerment within to feel, behave, and grow to be equal to men. At the same time, the archetype teaches men that acknowledging their weaknesses won't make them appear feminine. Followers of Dark Goddesses learn that both genders have much more to offer than those qualities traditionally ascribed to them. Despite their best intention of not harming anyone, no one embodies this "perfect" quality. It's not possible to never make a mistake or hurt anyone. *If nothing else, you'll eventually hurt yourself.*

It's not uncommon for Dark Goddesses to be shown as opportunistic and vengeful, especially when it comes to punishing mortals. Yet, true followers know that while they are easily angered, the wrath of a Dark Goddess is never undeserved or without a cause. Some people just need a bigger push (or a powerful lesson) to embrace and understand their relation to themselves and every other being in the universe. Albeit in an unusual way, the goddesses teach empathy for everything and everyone around you, as well as for yourself. The only way to learn the former lesson is to start with the latter. Whether you identify with a goddess who represents transformation or a warrior sorceress, you can be sure she will show you how to embrace your own values and character. The resonance you feel within is key to working with any archetype, and this is no different for the Dark Goddess, either.

In some representations, the Dark Goddess archetype is the result of the unification of two opposing energies. The followers of these concepts rely on similar beliefs to Jung's model - the person is a whole made of two opposites within themselves. Likewise, practitioners of these traditions believe that by uniting the two divine powers, a new, more powerful divine energy is born. Unlike in other cultures, where the archetype is portrayed as something that undermines other forces (even benevolent divine ones), here, the goddess is emphatic and noble, capable of recognizing the need for balance in nature. This balance dictates that where there is light, there must be dark. Therefore, the opposing divine forces are both necessary and equal. While portrayed as fearsome and relentless, Dark Goddesses display an excellence of personal character - it's only a question of recognizing it. They are brave and courageous and ready to confront anyone they need to in the pursuit of winning the battle.

Those dabbling in alchemy and similar alternative practices believe that embracing the Dark Goddess archetype leads to a radical transformation, after which a person is better equipped to discover and cultivate empathy, love, and strength. While some of these qualities are not typically associated with dark female energies, the many representations of the archetype show that evoking Dark Goddesses often results in acquiring them and achieving personal and spiritual growth. By learning empathy when working with a Dark Goddess, one becomes more capable of understanding not only their own shortcomings but others' as well. After all, who better to teach you about acceptance than someone who is considered terrifying, deadly, and unapproachable? If you can accept them as they are, you can embrace your and other people's true personalities, whether they are sensed as terrible, awesome, relatable, unanimous, or in any other way.

In most cultures, the Dark Goddess archetype represents something inexplicable, intangible, and uncontrollable. This is another superb reason why working with them potentially benefits every spiritual seeker or even advanced practitioner. Often, what can be ascribed to these qualities is considered bad or evil - including parts of yourself. You have all these values within you, reminding you of your interconnectedness with everything in nature. Working with a Dark Goddess makes all of these seem more real and tangible. Many believe that archetypes can help deal with the unforeseen - many of the Dark Goddesses' actions were seen as such across the different myths and beliefs.

Those who previously feared the chaotic unknown that lies within them learned after working with a Dark Goddess (or the archetype itself) that just because there is something they didn't know about themselves, it doesn't mean they have to fear it. In contemporary portrayals, this archetype of dark feminine power became an indispensable tool for self-development. Besides dissuading your fears from the hidden parts of yourself, the Dark Goddesses can show you how to integrate them into your conscious psyche.

The Dark Goddess archetype symbolizes a more profound yet challenging side of people's existence, forces that shaped lives since the beginning of time. While interpretations and symbolism of these divine female energies vary across beliefs, these infinite variations are the reason people with individual needs can identify themselves with them. You can find your own way to work with one or more Dark Goddesses and embark on an eventful journey of discovery.

# Chapter 2: Greek Goddesses

While the names of goddesses like Hera, who's known for being the queen of the gods, and Athena, the wise and strategic goddess of wisdom and warfare, roll off people's tongues effortlessly, there are some other intriguing, less well-recognized figures in Greek mythology. Persephone, Nyx, and Hekate are among them. These Dark Goddesses often bear the label of 'dark' or 'evil,' but understanding their origins and stories can shed light on their true natures.

Persephone, for example, is linked to the changing of seasons. Her tale begins with her being whisked away to the underworld by Hades, where she becomes his wife. This myth symbolizes the cycle of nature, where life goes through periods of dormancy and renewal. In the spring, Persephone returns to the Earth's surface, bringing with her the blossoms and beauty of the season. So, she's not really evil. She's more of a symbol of nature's perpetual cycle.

These Dark Goddesses often bear the label of "dark"', but understanding their stories can shed light on their true natures.²

Nyx, the goddess of night, is a much older deity than the more famous Olympian gods and goddesses. She's the mother of several essential concepts, like Sleep and Death. Nyx isn't evil. She embodies the tranquility and rest that the night provides. Her dark embrace is a time for recharging and renewal.

Hekate, the goddess of crossroads, magic, and witchcraft, is another misunderstood figure. In ancient Greece, people invoked her at a crossroads to seek guidance and protection from evil spirits. Her association with magic sometimes led to her being portrayed as a sinister figure. However, she's a symbol of the knowledge and power found in the unknown and the choices you make in life.

These goddesses aren't truly evil or dark in the way you might think of villains. They represent different facets of life, like change, the mysteries of night, and the hidden wisdom within the world. They add layers of meaning to Greek mythology, and by exploring their stories, you can get a deeper appreciation for the complexities of life and nature. This chapter will help you explore the world of these dark Greek goddesses, especially from an esoteric perspective.

With so much literature available today, it's hard to separate the original stories from modified ones. However, learning how these goddesses were actually understood in their ancient context explains their significance and place. So, read on to unravel the hidden truths and untold tales of Persephone, Nyx, Hekate, and their mysterious counterparts, shedding light on the enigmatic and captivating aspects of Greek mythology that have long remained in the shadows.

# Hecate/Hekate

Hekate, the goddess of crossroads, magic, and witchcraft.[8]

Hekate, the goddess of crossroads, magic, and witchcraft, has an ancient and mysterious history. She is one of the Titans, a group of primordial deities that predate the Olympian gods and goddesses. Her parents were Perses and Asteria, and she was often depicted as a triple goddess, representing the moon's three phases: the maiden, the mother, and the crone. This symbolism connects her to the cycles of life and the mysteries of the universe.

One of the most famous stories about Hekate centers on her role in the Titanomachy, the epic battle between the Titans and the Olympian gods. Hekate chose to remain neutral in this conflict, and, as a result, she was one of the few Titans to avoid imprisonment in the underworld after the Titans were defeated. Her neutrality and her ability to navigate the liminal spaces between light and dark, life and death, made her a unique and enigmatic figure.

Hekate's association with Crossroads is a central point of her mythology. In ancient Greece, travelers would often place offerings at crossroads to seek her protection and guidance. She was believed to have the power to open the gates between the mortal world and the spirit realm. This connection to crossroads symbolizes choices and transitions in life, emphasizing her role as a guide through life's uncertainties.

Hekate is also closely linked to magic and witchcraft. In the ancient world, she was often invoked during rituals and spells, particularly those associated with the moon and the night. Her torches illuminated the path in the darkness, both physically and metaphorically, guiding those who sought her wisdom and protection. She was considered a guardian of the mysteries of the occult, and her followers believed she could grant them knowledge and power. There are many myths surrounding this magical goddess, some of these include:

### 1. Hekate and the Abduction of Persephone

One of the most well-known myths involving Hekate is her role in the abduction of Persephone by Hades, which led to the changing seasons. According to the myth, Hades, the god of the underworld, fell in love with Persephone, the daughter of Demeter, the goddess of agriculture (more to be discussed later). When Hades abducted Persephone, Demeter was grief-stricken and wandered the Earth in search of her daughter. With her torches, Hekate helped Demeter in her search and played a crucial role in the reunion of mother and daughter. This myth highlights Hekate's connection to the underworld and her role as a guide in the realm of the dead.

## 2. The Role of Hekate in the Trojan War

Hekate also appears in the context of the Trojan War. She was believed to have aided the Greeks by providing them with guidance and protection during their long journey to Troy. The famous sorceress Medea, who was a priestess of Hekate, was said to have invoked the goddess's powers in her magical practices, demonstrating Hekate's role as a deity associated with magic and witchcraft.

## 3. Hekate's Encounter with Theseus

In another myth, the hero, Theseus, encountered Hekate when he was on his way to fight the Minotaur in the labyrinth. Hekate provided Theseus with guidance and protection during his perilous journey. She lit his path with her torches and offered him wisdom, ensuring his safe return from the labyrinth after defeating the Minotaur.

## 4. Hekate and the Dogs

Hekate is often illustrated accompanied by dogs, and in Greek mythology, it was believed that the sound of howling dogs was a sign of her presence. Dogs were considered sacred to her and often sacrificed in her rituals. Some myths even suggest that Hekate could transform into a dog, further emphasizing her close connection with these animals.

## 5. Hekate's Role in the Perseus and Medusa Myth

Hekate played a significant part in the tale of Perseus and Medusa. She assisted Perseus on his quest to slay the Gorgon Medusa. Hekate provided him with a polished shield to use as a mirror, enabling him to approach Medusa without directly looking at her and turning to stone. This myth underscores her association with powerful magical artifacts and her willingness to support heroes in their quests.

## 6. Hekate and the Protection of Newborns

Hekate was also revered as a protector of newborns and was often invoked during childbirth. It was believed that she could ward off evil spirits and ensure a safe delivery. Mothers would call upon Hekate to safeguard their infants during the vulnerable period of birth.

## 7. Hekate's Nightly Walks

Another intriguing belief about Hekate was that she was known to roam the Earth at night, particularly during the dark moon. During these nightly journeys, she was thought to be accompanied by a procession of restless spirits and the howling of dogs. People would leave offerings at crossroads to appease and seek her blessings during these nighttime excursions.

## 8. Hekate and the Golden Fleece

In the quest for the Golden Fleece, Hekate's assistance was sought by Jason and the Argonauts. It is said that she gave them knowledge and guidance to navigate the treacherous waters and challenges they encountered on their epic journey. This myth highlights her role as a source of wisdom and aid for heroes.

## 9. Hekate's Involvement in Orpheus' Quest

In the myth of Orpheus and Eurydice, when Orpheus descended into the underworld to rescue his beloved Eurydice, Hekate was one of the deities he encountered. Her presence in the underworld signified her influence over the realm of the dead and her role in guiding souls.

## 10. Hekate's Association with the Eumenides

Hekate was often linked with the Eumenides, also known as the Furies, who were vengeful spirits associated with the punishment of wrongdoers. Hekate acted as a mediator between the Eumenides and those who sought to appease them, reflecting her role as an intermediary between the human and divine realms.

Hekate, the goddess associated with the night, the dead, crossroads, and magic, is often viewed as a dark and enigmatic figure in Greek mythology. Her realm encompasses many elements that could be interpreted as mysterious and even foreboding, including her association with the occult, the spirit world, and the unseen forces of the cosmos. However, it is essential to recognize that Hekate was never inherently evil or malevolent, as her stories and deeds demonstrate.

Throughout Greek mythology and literature, Hekate consistently emerges as a guide, a protector, and a source of wisdom. She played pivotal roles in numerous heroic quests, aiding and offering insight to those who sought her assistance. Whether it was helping Perseus confront Medusa, guiding Jason in the quest for the Golden Fleece, or assisting

Aeneas in his journey to the underworld, Hekate showcased her benevolent side as a goddess who aided and protected those in need.

Hekate's connection to magic is often misunderstood. While she is associated with the mystical arts, it is crucial to remember that magic, like any tool, is not inherently good or evil; it depends on the intentions and actions of those who practice it. In her role as a guardian of magic, Hekate is neither good nor evil but is a source of knowledge and power for those who seek her guidance.

In essence, Hekate is a goddess of duality, representing the balance between light and dark, life and death, and the known and the unknown. Her mysteries and her multifaceted character reveal the complexities of existence, where she acts as a guiding force for those who find themselves at the crossroads of life.

# Persephone

Persephone, the bringer of destruction.'

Persephone, the daughter of Demeter, the goddess of agriculture, and Zeus, the king of the gods, was a radiant and joyful young goddess. Her name, which means "bringer of destruction" or "bringer of death," foreshadows her eventual transformation into a dark deity. She was often described as a symbol of the bountiful Earth, radiating life and growth wherever she went.

Before her fateful encounter with Hades, Persephone enjoyed a carefree and idyllic life with her mother, Demeter. She spent her days in the meadows, nurturing the growth of flowers and crops, spreading beauty and abundance across the land. Her laughter and joy were said to have the power to make flowers bloom and fields flourish.

Persephone's abduction by Hades was a violent and sudden event. The earth literally cracked open, and Hades, in his dark chariot, emerged to seize her. Persephone's screams for help went unanswered as Hades took her to the depths of the underworld against her will. The stark element of her story is the contrast between her previous life in the bright, sunlit world and her abrupt descent into the shadowy realm of death.

Persephone's initial despair in the underworld is evident. She longed for her mother and the world above. However, as time passed, she assumed her role as the queen of the dead. She became a compassionate figure, bestowing solace to the souls in the afterlife. Her presence in the underworld signifies her strength and adaptability as she embraces her new role despite the initial hardship.

As Persephone was whisked away by Hades to the depths of the underworld, the world above mourned her absence. Her mother, Demeter, the goddess of agriculture, was grief-stricken. Consumed by despair, Demeter allowed the Earth to wither and the crops to die, and famine threatened the mortal realm.

1. **Demeter's Quest to Find Her Daughter**

    Demeter, in her anguish, embarked on a relentless quest to find her beloved daughter. She searched high and low, appealing to the other gods for assistance. However, none could reveal Persephone's whereabouts, for it was a secret known only to the lord of the underworld.

2. **Zeus' Intervention**

    Seeing the suffering of both the gods and mortals due to the barrenness of the Earth, Zeus, the king of the gods, intervened. He urged Hades to release Persephone, recognizing that her return to the surface world was essential to ending the famine.

### 3. The Compromise with the Pomegranate Seeds

Hades agreed to allow Persephone to return but presented a single condition. Since she had consumed six pomegranate seeds in the underworld, it was decreed that she must spend six months of each year with Hades. These months coincided with the winter season, during which the world would be shrouded in cold and darkness.

### 4. Persephone's Return and the Changing Seasons

Upon her return to the world above, Persephone's joyful reunion with her mother, Demeter, marked the beginning of spring. The Earth burst into life as flowers bloomed and crops flourished. The world reveled in the rebirth of nature and the return of Persephone.

### 5. The Waning of Life in the Underworld

During her absence from the underworld, the spirits of the dead longed for Persephone's return. The realm of the dead felt a waning of life and vitality as they missed the queen who offered them comfort and solace.

Persephone's story became a symbol of the eternal cycle of the seasons. Her time with Hades in the underworld marked the arrival of winter and the dormancy of the earth. Her reunions with Demeter aboveground signaled the renewal of life and the return of spring and summer.

Persephone's story reflects her dual nature. She is both the goddess of spring and growth when she is with her mother, Demeter, and the queen of the underworld during her time with Hades. This duality embodies the cycle of the seasons, with her descent into the underworld marking the arrival of winter and her return signifying the rebirth of spring.

### Persephone as a Dark Goddess

Persephone's association with the underworld and her role as queen of the dead contribute to her reputation as a Dark Goddess. She is not evil, but her realm is one of shadows, death, and mystery. Her transformation from a carefree maiden into a powerful and enigmatic queen of the underworld underscores her dark aspect. Persephone's story also serves as a reminder of the delicate balance between life and death in the natural world.

Despite her dark associations, Persephone is not a malevolent deity. She is often depicted as a compassionate and fair ruler in the underworld, balancing the scales of justice and providing comfort to souls in the afterlife. Her annual return to the surface world heralds the rebirth of life and nature, symbolizing the cycle of renewal and growth.

## Nyx

Nyx, a goddess as old as time itself, emerged from Chaos, the primeval void from which the entire cosmos came forth. She was the embodiment of the night, the personification of darkness, and one of the original deities that predated even the mighty Olympian gods. She was a goddess of great depth, a figure of profound beauty veiled in an aura of darkness. Her dominion extended far beyond the physical night. She governed the abstract concepts associated with darkness, making her a deity of immense influence. In the realm of night, she presided over sleep, dreams, and even death.

One of the most fascinating aspects of Nyx was her many and diverse offspring. Among her notable children was Hypnos, the god of sleep, known for bringing rest and dreams to mortals. Another was Thanatos, the personification of death, representing the peaceful transition from life to the afterlife. Moros, the god of impending doom, underscored the inescapable fate that awaited all beings. Eris, the goddess of strife, thrived in the shadows, sowing discord and

Nyx emerged from Chaos.[5]

conflict often concealed under the cover of darkness. Apate, the deity of deceit, and Geras, representing the inevitable march of old age, were other offspring of Nyx. This diversity of her children emphasized the complexity of the forces Nyx presided over.

Nyx's presence in Greek mythology was all-pervasive, even though she did not feature as prominently as some other deities. She was often invoked during nighttime rituals when the world was shrouded in the mysteries of the dark. Nyx held immense power in her dominion over transitions, presiding over the shift from wakefulness to sleep, from life to death, and from consciousness to the ethereal world of dreams. Her influence was not only over the physical night but extended into the depths of the subconscious, the realm of dreams, and the enigmatic forces that governed existence. She was the true representation of a Dark Goddess.

In Greek mythology, there are some well-known and powerful goddesses like Athena and Aphrodite, but not much is said about the darker goddesses such as Nyx, Persephone, and Hekate. These figures are often associated with mystery and darkness, which might make people think they're evil. However, as you've explored their stories in this chapter, it's clear that they aren't necessarily evil. These Dark Goddesses are more complex than just being considered evil. Their stories reveal Greek mythology's depth and intricacy, showing that labels like "dark" or "evil" can be too simplistic to describe these multifaceted goddesses.

# Chapter 3: Egyptian Goddesses

When one thinks of ancient Egyptian deities, only a few come to mind, like Cleopatra, Nefertiti, and Tutankhamun. However, there are many other gods and goddesses with fascinating powers and intriguing stories that you have probably never heard about before, like Sekhmet, Nephthys, Hathor, and Nut, the ancient Egyptian Dark Goddess.

Ancient Egyptian Dark Goddess.[6]

# Sekhmet

Sekhmet means "One who is in control" or "She who is powerful." It is a fitting name for one of the most powerful goddesses in ancient Egyptian mythology. She is referred to as the Mother Goddess and is part human, part animal. She is depicted as a woman with the face of a lion. There are many sculptures, amulets, and other monuments of Sekhmet which show her significance in ancient Egypt.

Sekhmet is a forgotten esoteric goddess. Esoteric deities have extraordinary abilities. So why is she a forgotten one? Sadly, not much is known about her, and she isn't mentioned in mythology as much as other deities. She remains an enigma. However, the few resources found about her praise her great but contradictory abilities. She could bring disease, chaos, and death while also administering healing and protection.

## Mythology

Sekhmet was the daughter of the sun god Ra, the creator of the universe. In one legend, she was an incarnation of the sky goddess Hathor. After Ra created mankind, he observed them from the skies. He had high hopes for his new creation, but he was disappointed to find they steered away from the right path and stopped following his rules of justice and order. He decided to punish them for their disobedience. He created Sekhmet from the fire in his eyes, which is why she is referred to as "The Eye of Ra." She was a weapon and a vengeful manifestation of his power that could breathe a fire hotter than the desert sun.

Ra sent Sekhmet to Earth to exact his punishment on mankind. She caused plagues across the lands. Using her fiery breath, Sekhmet set everything in her way on fire, killing almost all of mankind. Her bloodlust was out of control, and no one could stop her. Ra regretted his decision when he saw what his daughter did to his creation. He wasn't cruel or heartless. He only wanted to punish them and had no intention of killing

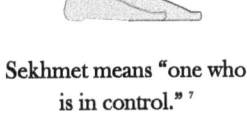

Sekhmet means "one who is in control." [7]

them. If all mankind was destroyed, who would learn the lesson?

Ra commanded some of his priests to get red ochre and grind it with beer. They then poured it all over the land at night while Sekhmet was sleeping.

Sekhmet, who was bloodthirsty, mistook the red beer for blood and drank it all. She got intoxicated and fell asleep. When she woke up, she returned to Ra. In one legend, this was when he made her the goddess of war and chaos.

**Attributes**

Sekhmet is the goddess of war, chaos, healing, plague, and the hot desert sun. She is described in the Book of the Dead as a destructive and creative force. She has the power to bring plagues to mankind. As a healing goddess, she could be invoked to protect against diseases. There isn't a problem Sekhmet couldn't fix. She is the patron of healers and physicians. During wars, Sekhmet was the protector of the pharaohs and led them to victory.

Sekhmet has about 4,000 names that reflect her personality and attributes.

- Watcher and guardian of the West.
- Lady of the mountains.
- Lady of the Fire (because she breathes fire and protects the sun god, Ra).
- Lady of bright red linen (reflecting her bloodlust).
- Mistress of Ankh Tawy (another name for Memphis, the capital of ancient Egypt).
- Mistress of the tombs (reflecting her role as the Dark Goddess).
- Mistress of dread (for almost destroying mankind).
- The bloodthirsty.
- Lady of life (for her healing powers).
- Red lady (for sending plagues to mankind).

**Roles**

Sekhmet is responsible for bringing heat to the deserts, and she is called "Nesert," meaning flame. She brings suffering and disease but only to those who anger her. She guards Ra and also protects Ma'at, the goddess of balance and justice. Because of her fierce and terrifying nature, Sekhmet is called the "Lady of Terror."

## Symbols

- Lioness
- Red linen
- Sun disk
- Cats

## Sekhmet, the Dark Goddess

In ancient times, everyone feared Sekhmet, for she was the goddess of war. However, she is only threatening to those who disrespected her. She protected the ancient Egyptians by breathing fire and killing their enemies. However, when in battle, Sekhmet becomes blinded with rage and destroys everything in her way. Only drinking blood could calm her fiery anger.

## Rituals/Worship

If you want to appease Sekhmet, burn incense, play music, or offer her food and drink.

## Meditation Ritual

### Instructions:

1. Build an altar for Sekhmet and place her pictures or symbols on its surface.
2. Light one or more candles.
3. Sit next to the altar in a comfortable position and close your eyes.
4. Take a few deep breaths and visualize Sekhmet.
5. Give yourself time until she either appears to you or you see any of her symbols.
6. Ask her for guidance.

# Nephthys

Nephthys is one of the first Egyptian goddesses. She was born from the union between the Sky and the Earth after Ra created the universe. Nephthys is her Latin name, and her Egyptian name is *Nebthwt*, meaning "Mistress of the House" or "The Lady of the Temple."

## Mythology

Osiris was the god of agriculture and fertility, and his wife, Isis, was the goddess of magic and light. They ruled over mankind together, and they were just and kind. Their sister, Nephthys, was married to their brother Set, the god of war. However, Nephthys had feelings for Osiris. One day, she transformed into Isis and seduced him, and they slept together. When Set found out, he thought that Osiris seduced and tricked Nephthys. Set already hated his brother and was very jealous of him, but after this incident, he planned to murder him. Set succeeded in his plan and killed his brother. He took his place as king with Nephthys by his side.

Isis was heartbroken over the loss of her husband and looked for his body everywhere. She wanted to bring him back to life so she could have his child. When she finally found him, she asked Nephthys to protect him from their evil brother, Set. However, Set figured out their plan and confronted Nephthys, who told him where they hid the body. Set took Osiris's body, cut it into little pieces, and threw them across the land.

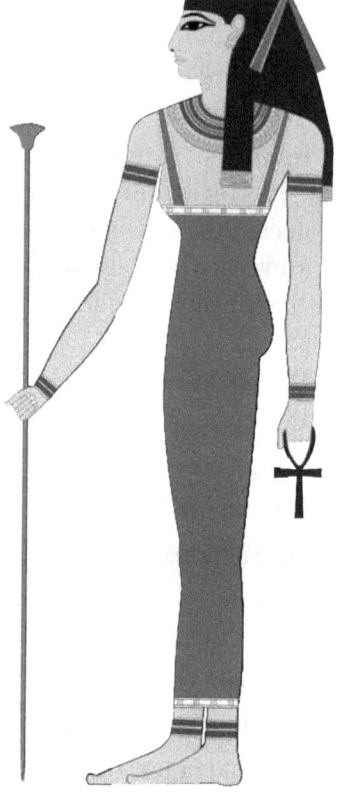

Nephthys is one of the first Egyptian goddesses.'

When Isis returned, Nephthys felt guilty for betraying her trust. She promised to do everything in her power to fix her mistake. The sisters managed to find Osiris's parts and put him back together. They brought him back to life, and Isis got pregnant and had a son called Horus.

She kept him hidden away from Set. Nephthys, who learned from her mistake, didn't reveal her sister's secret to anyone. She nursed Horus and helped Isis raise him. When Horus grew up and took back his throne, he made Nephthys the head of his family and his chief counselor. Because of this myth, many Egyptians consider Nephthys a nursing mother and a symbol of guidance and protection.

### Attributes

Nephthys is depicted as a woman with the symbol of her name over her head. Her illustrations were present in many ancient tombs because she protected the dead and attended Osiris's mummification.

### Roles

She is associated with darkness, twilight, and the setting sun. She is the goddess of the air, sky, heaven, and hell. She protects the dead from evil spirits by transforming into a kite and wails to mourn the departed. She guarded the coffins and the canopic jars where the deceased organs were stored. She originally protected Hapi, god of the Nile, jars but later became protector of all containers.

### Symbols

- Sycamore trees
- Temples
- Hawks
- Glacons
- Woman with wings.
- Kites
- Beer

### Nephthys, the Dark Goddess

Nephthys is the goddess of death and is associated with decay. She helps the souls of the departed cross over to the other side. She takes care of these spirits even after she escorts them to the afterlife. She comforts their families during their mourning period and lets them know that their loved ones are safe and in a good place. This is why she is called "Friend of the Dead." In fact, she is the only goddess to care about the dead and treat them with love and kindness.

Her followers often call on her after the death of a loved one, so she is present during funerals to guard the dead. Nephthys has magical abilities that resemble Isis, the goddess of magic and healing. Isis is a force of light, and Nephthys is a force of darkness, so they balance each other.

Nephthys also became the goddess of birth after giving birth to Anubis, the god of death.

### Rituals/Worship

Invoke Nephthys with his visualization technique.

1. Find a quiet room and sit in a comfortable position.
2. Close your eyes and put your hands together, then place them on your heart.
3. Take a long, deep breath and visualize the light of Nephthys flowing through every part of your body.
4. Breathe out and feel her light beneath your feet.
5. Take a long, deep breath and feel her light filling your heart.
6. Vibrate her name, then slowly open your hands and let her light fill your space.
7. If you feel her presence, ask her any question you have.
8. After you have finished, express your gratitude to her.

# Hathor

Hathor is associated with Sekhmet, and some historians believe that Sekhmet is derived from her. She is depicted either as a cow or a woman with a cow's head. Hathor is Ra's daughter and was highly venerated among the ancient Egyptians. Her name means "Temple of Horus," which refers to how Horus (the sun god) enters her mouth every night to sleep and then wakes up the next morning to light the sky. This myth explains how the sun shines and sets every day.

### Mythology

Hathor was an image of love and kindness. However, before that, she used to have a much darker side. In some legends, Ra sent Hathor to punish mankind for their disobedience. After she unleashed her vengeance and destroyed everything and everyone, as a result of her evil doings, she transformed into Sekhmet. When she woke up from this intoxication, she was back to being Hathor. However, she had changed and became a

Hathor's name means "Temple of Horus." '

better, kinder, and calmer version of herself.

The goddess who wanted to annihilate the world became an ally to mankind. She blessed them with many gifts and helped the less fortunate. Whenever they prayed to her, she would come through for them. She became the mother goddess, and all the other goddesses are believed to be her avatars.

In another myth, when Horus grew up, he wanted to claim the throne from his uncle Set. Since Set was cunning and untrustworthy, Horus took his case to the counsel of gods who were led by Ra. However, Ra couldn't see eye to eye with one of the gods. So, he became angry and refused to participate in the trial.

Hathor knew that her father's anger could bring the end of the world. So she visited him, and in an unexpected move, she revealed her genitals. He was amused and aroused, and his anger subsided. He then went back to court to handle Horus's case.

This story highlights the significance of masculinity and femininity. When both are in harmony, they bring balance to the universe.

### Attributes

Hathor is the goddess of love, celebration, music, dance, motherhood, gratitude, drunkenness, and joy, similar to Venus and Aphrodite from Roman and Greek mythology. She is also the patron of women and their health.

She is also the ruler of childbirth, the East, the West, fertility, agriculture, the moon, the sun, and the sky.

### Roles

Hathor has many different roles. She is responsible for renewing the cosmos, helping women give birth, and resurrecting the dead. She is also a lunar deity and guides the boats at night till they reach the shore safely. In ancient Egypt, night was a metaphor for death. So, it is also believed that she illuminates the way for the deceased to reach their final resting place.

### Symbols

- Cow
- Cow's ears
- Cow horns
- Solar disk

- Papyrus plant
- Sycamore tree
- Serpent
- Lioness

### Hathor the Dark Goddess

Hathor holds the great honor of being the goddess of the afterlife in The Field of Reeds. It is a place similar to the concept of paradise where the dead spend their eternity with their loved ones without any pain or suffering.

When a good woman or girl dies, she assumes the likeness of Hathor before crossing to the Field of Reeds.

### Rituals/Worship

Connect with Hathor by making any of these offerings:

- Roses
- Cedar
- Cinnamon
- Myrrh
- Wine
- Beer
- Butter
- Cheese
- Bread
- Dates
- Figs
- Freshwater
- Jasmine, chamomile, or rose oil.
- Perfumes
- Gold
- Copper

You can also set an altar in her honor. Keep the decoration simple; a picture or statue of her and a red or white candle will be enough.

# Nut

Nut is the daughter of Shu, the god of air, and Tenfut, the goddess of rainfall and moisture. She is Ra's granddaughter and married to Geb, the god of the earth. Nut is the goddess of the sky and one of the most significant deities in ancient mythology.

The name "Nut" means water, and she is depicted with a water pot on her head.

## Mythology

When Ra created Nut (the sky) and Geb (the earth), they were close and had non-stop sex. They were unable to let each other go. Although their love was so strong, this closeness prevented Nut from having children. Geb and Nut's father, Shu, wanted her to give birth to his grandchildren. He was also jealous of Geb and Nut's close relationship, so he forced them to separate. This was how the separation of the sky and Earth was explained in ancient Egyptian mythology.

In another myth, Ra loved Nut and wanted to marry her. However, she was in love with Geb and they were sleeping together. When Ra found out, he cursed her so she could never have children in any month of the year.

Nut went to Thoth, the god of wisdom, and sought his help. He was fond of her, so he devised a plan to help her break the curse.

Nut, the goddess of the sky.[10]

He challenged Koshnu, the goddess of the moon, to a game of checkers. They kept making bets and placing wagers on each match. Thoth won the game, and Koahnu gave him a part of her illumination. Thoth used it to add five extra days to the year. Since they didn't belong to any month, Nut was able to cheat Ra's curse. She gave birth to Osiris, Isis, Seth, and Nephthys.

Nut also helped Ra ascend to the sky. Ra decided to abdicate his throne and retire to the skies. However, he was so old and weak and couldn't make the journey on his own. Nun asked Nut to carry Ra on her back and bring him to the skies. However, Ra was very large, and Nut didn't believe she could carry him by herself. So Nun transformed her into a cow that Ra rode and reached the skies.

### Attributes
Nut is depicted as a beautiful naked woman with wings standing in the skies and is covered in drawings of stars.

### Roles
Nut protects the world from Nun, the water of creation. She also gave birth to four members of the Great Enneads. They were the first nine gods in ancient Egyptian mythology: Ra, Shu, Tefnut, Geb, Nut, Osiris, Isis, Seth, and Nephthys.

She used to be the goddess of the night sky and was associated with the Milky Way. Over time, her role changed, and she became the goddess of all skies.

### Symbols
- Sky
- Cow
- Stars
- Freedom
- Omnipotence
- Wisdom
- Abundance
- Eternity
- Immortality
- Frogs
- Bunnies
- Bees
- Lotus flowers
- Opal
- Blue Topaz
- Tourmaline
- Sapphire
- Blue
- Black

### The Dark Goddess Aspect

Nut is the goddess of sarcophagi and coffins. She watches over the dead until their rebirth in the afterlife.

### Rituals/Worship

Practice this ritual if you want to invoke Nut.

1. Choose a place outdoors under the night sky, or you can set up an indoor altar with night symbols like stars, constellations, or the moon.
2. Light a white or blue candle.
3. Place any of Nut's symbols on the altar.
4. Make an offering to Nut.
5. Meditate next to the altar by closing your eyes and focusing on your breathing.
6. Clear your mind and visualize Nut.
7. Ask her for guidance and be ready to receive her wisdom.

### Nut and Kemetic Spirituality

Kemetic spirituality is a belief inspired by ancient Egyptian religion that focuses on the connection between mankind and the divine and the belief that the universe is an extension of yourself.

The ancient religion is based on the circle of life that Nut represents. Every night, she swallows the sun god and then gives birth to him the next morning. She also swallows the moon every morning and gives birth to her at night.

The dark ancient Egyptian goddesses embody a number of characteristics. They can be bloodthirsty and a force of destruction and also guides and protectors. They represent a complex, multi-faced nature of ancient Egyptian mythology, where light and darkness and creation and destruction are intertwined in a complex cosmic tapestry.

# Chapter 4: Mesopotamian Goddesses

In this chapter, you'll find an in-depth exploration of the Mesopotamian Dark Goddesses, Ereshkigal, Lilith, and Inanna. Besides examining the different aspects of the divine feminine, as expressed through their mythology, roles, and qualities, you'll also learn about their symbol as a Dark Goddess.

## Lilith

Lilith appears in numerous cultures and traditions.[11]

Also known as Lillake, Lilitu, Belili, and Baalat, Lilith appears in numerous cultures and traditions. Her most prominent role is tied to Jewish mythology, which claims she was Adam's first wife. According to the tale, Lilith refused to submit to her husband's wishes because she believed they should be equal. As a result, she left Adam but was cursed to bear only demons instead of children. Some claim that she later returned to the paradise she abandoned, turned herself into a snake and caused Adam and his new wife, Eve, to be expelled too. However, the origins of this myth can be traced back to the Sumero-Babylonian Goddess who had the same dark and frivolous qualities as she is given in the rabbinical tales. Here, too, Lilith is described as a screeching demon, either accompanied by an owl or turning into one, lurking during the night and attacking unsuspecting men and children. Since she can't have her own children, she takes her fury out on others by killing them. The Canaanites, on the other hand, held her in high regard, addressing her as the "Divine Lady." Perhaps it was the combination of all these myths that led to the emergence of Lilith as the goddess of rebellion, independence, and innate sexuality.

One of her earliest mentions is on a clay tablet from Ur, dating back to 2000 B.C., but based on mythology, her roots can be traced back to Sumer, 3000 B.C. Later folklore puts her origins at a much earlier date, in 700 B.C., when she was first called Lilith, the name under which she is known today. In some Babylonian legends, Lilith is known as the Maid of Desolation or Dark Maid. She either works with the creatures of the night, terrorizing people or is one of them (as a vampire or demon). Despite her demonlike features, claws, and bird feet, she is so beautiful and enchanting that no man who encounters her can resist her. In rituals, Lilith can be represented by red jasper, garnet, carnelian, or any other orange or red crystals that convey passion and sensuality.

According to a Sumerian Legend, Lilith was jealous of Inanna, the goddess of war and love. When Inanna planted a sacred tree she wanted to make her throne, Lilith flew onto the tree in a bird form, preventing Inanna from taking residence. Some claim Lilith's actions were deliberate attempts to obstruct Inanna from reaching her full power (Innana was afraid of birds, and Lilith knew she wouldn't dare to go on a tree occupied by a bird). However, the hero Gilgamesh comes to Inanna's rescue, driving Lilith out and enabling Innana to take her rightful place.

Due to her sexual symbolism, in Ancient Mesopotamian culture, Lilith is also associated with breasts. Being a powerful female demon, Lilith is said to cause diseases affecting women, preventing them from breastfeeding their children and causing them to die. This is likely related to her inability to bear and nurse children, which may have driven her to want to prevent other women from doing the same.

As an archetype of an empowering Dark Goddess, Lilith is seen as the goddess of Wild Freedom. She teaches her followers that they must be willing to embrace who they truly are and trust that those who are meant to accept them will come in time. While she acknowledged that this is sometimes easier said than done, she encourages everyone to maintain self-sovereignty even when they're shamed and cast aside for their thoughts, feelings, or actions. No outside validation is worth sacrificing who you are within or abandoning the love you have for yourself.

Moreover, Lilith teaches her followers that instead of submitting to others' will and needs, they become the ones who hold and uplift those who are pushed aside by society. She encourages them to devote themselves to a fierce passion that supports their tender quality instead of suffocating it. In a sense, Lilith is one of the most rewarding Dark Goddesses to work with as she helps worshippers become closer to the divine feminine archetype they identify with.

At the same time, Lilith doesn't discourage anyone from completely disregarding their loved ones' needs. She fosters raising one's standard instead and finding a way to appreciate these demands while taking care of one's own needs. She teaches how to make the seed of a woman's inner wisdom and values blossom, finding balance in this world full of diversity. Lilith acknowledges that ambivalent feelings toward meeting one's needs are born from an inner dark void.

This dark aspect of Lilith seems dangerous and intense, but it doesn't have to be. While it's true that following this dark feminine power can generate many negative experiences, it's necessary in order to find a balance in life. Lilith can drive you to seek conflicts without a valid reason (other than seeking attention), become irritated with everyone who expresses different points of view, become domineering, selfish, and boastful, and disregard other people's needs. In modern terms, she is like a psychic vampire (an apt name given her portrayal in mythology), draining people of energy and the will to live. You need to exercise extreme caution to prevent yourself from falling into the trap of disregarding her positive lessons and using her power for selfish reasons.

Whether seen as a mixture of light and dark or a completely dark one, in all cultures she appeared, Lilith seems to provide a form of liberation to those she encountered. For example, by seducing men, as described in Mesopotamian mythology, she gave them a sense of uninhibited freedom from moral constraints. While some may argue that her methods were exceedingly radical, they have been shown to be necessary to make people face the consequences they were unprepared or unwilling to handle.

## Inanna

Inanna is known by Sumerians as "the lady of the heavens."[13]

Known by the Sumerians as "the lady of the heavens," Inanna is one of the most complex and mysterious of all dark deities. She is thought to be the daughter of Ningal and Anu and the twin sister of Ereshkigal, another Dark Goddess from Mesopotamian mythology. In some myths, Inanna is pushed into an arranged marriage to Dumuzi, while in others, she is unmarried, and Dumuzi is only her consort. Either way, she was keen to maintain her boundaries with him, which went against her temptress aura in the Epic of Gilgamesh, where she wanted to take the hero who saved her as a lover but was rejected by him.

Inanna's traits are just as contradictory as the tales about her actions and roles. Known by many as an influential, ambitious, and empowering goddess, she also seems to be a shy maiden whose potential and freedom are restricted by the patriarchal society she lives in. There is, however, a focal point in all of her stories, and this is her sexuality. Her sensual nature is evident in various pieces of Mesopotamian poetry and tales, with people praying to her when they needed help with impotence or unrequited love. Some even went as far as claiming her to be the patron of the ladies of the night.

Inanna is also associated with art and is often illustrated in art pieces nude or wearing a cape and slightly revealing her nude figure underneath. By contrast, in other depictions, she is wearing a trimmed robe and has weapons peeking out from under her shoulders, indicating her passion for warfare. She may also hold a weapon in her hands and even be illustrated with a beard to emphasize her masculinity, as it was believed that to be a successful leader in a battle, you had to be male.

Inanna's preference for military functions wasn't evident before the Old Akkadian period when scripts mainly focused on her femininity. Some theorize that the masculine and war-like aspects were used as additional leverage for exercising political power when her feminine nature wasn't enough to sway people over.

Innana is often represented by a bundle of reeds standing in front of two gate posts. She can also be seen standing on a lion's back. She is associated with the colors red and blue and the stones carnelian and lapis lazuli. Some claim that red and blue signify her feminine and masculine natures, respectively. An eight-pointed star is sometimes used to symbolize the goddess's transcendent nature.

According to a myth, Inanna was attacked by a gardener while she was sleeping under a tree. Infuriated, she embarked on a long journey to find the gardener who went into hiding. Her journey is often likened to that of Venus' astral path.

In another story, Inanna journeys to the underworld and back. There, she sits on Ereshkigal's throne, which angers the other deities in the pantheon, who then kill her for her insolence. After her helper, Ninšubur, asked for Enki's help, the two of them brought Inanna back to the world. Due to her trips back and forth from the world of the dead, Inanna became associated with the journey to the afterlife in Assyrian mythology.

However, because it is never that simple in mythology, other tales claim that Inanna only wanted to patch things up with her estranged sister and paid a high price for it. At the time it occurred to her to visit Ereshkigal in the underworld, Inanna was already a celebrated ruler and a celebrated goddess. She was blessed with beauty, power, and influence and seemingly had it all. Yet, after being at odds with her twin for so long, she was compelled to leave their differences behind. She felt she was denying parts of herself and needed to reclaim them. As she was traveling to the underworld, Inanna was stopped at each of the seven gates of the underworld. At each stop, she was stripped more and more of her possessions, powers, and parts of her identity. When finally reunited with her sister, Inanna wasn't a welcomed guest. Having just lost her husband, Ereshkigal wasn't in the mood to patch things up with her sister (although some tales claim that Ereshkigal's husband's death was caused by Inanna's actions). Wanting Inanna to leave her alone, Ereshkigal left her sister to die by hanging her up on a deadly hook. However, Inanna's guides traveled to the underworld and, after comforting Ereshkigal as she was mourning her husband, they convinced her to give Inanna's body back to them so they could take her back to the world of the living.

According to yet another version of the story, Inanna was revived by the red waters of life, emerging from the underworld with even more power and influence. It's unclear whether this power had been bestowed upon her deliberately by her twin or was a result of her revival from the dead. This version of Inanna's journey to the underworld relates most closely to her Dark Goddess archetype. As the dark feminine, she teaches her followers that there is a hidden desire to explore the repressed parts of the self in everyone. Sometimes, people don't understand what compels others to seek out the darkest parts of themselves or act in a way that results in the same.

As a Dark Goddess, Inanna encourages one to take one's own "Underworld Journey," exploring the deepest, most hidden parts that the ego doesn't want to acknowledge. Instead of layers of projection, understanding, and satisfaction with blanket truths about one's darkest traits, she fosters seeking them out, even if they lead to pain caused by the death of the ego. Just as Inanna was stripped of everything that kept her ego alive, so will everyone who confronts their shadow self. However, as these hidden pockets are often filled with repressed grief, exploring them can lay a foundation for healing in a healthy way.

It takes a truly courageous person to surrender more fully to the darkness without knowing what they will encounter. However, by illuminating these dark spaces, you can unravel negative emotions caused by past trauma, like shame, guilt, denial, and delusion of separation, and eventually unearth the empowering compassion. By embracing the darkest side she was compelled to explore, Inanna was able to reclaim her title among the living and emerge as an even more powerful queen and goddess than she was before. And just as she was able to gain empowerment by reclaiming everything within her, so can everyone who chooses to work with her as a Dark Goddess.

## Ereshkigal

Ereshkigal is the goddess of the underworld in Mesopotamian mythology. Being the ruler of the land of the dead, Ereshkigal is associated with death, transformation, and the mysteries of the afterlife. "Ereshkigal" translates to "Queen of the Great Place/Below." According to legend, while the souls who ended up in her realm ate dust and drank mud, Ereshkigal resided in a palace built of lapis lazuli, enticing the dead souls to come to her. Once they were in her realm, Ereshkigal kept the souls there and refused to release them. Some claimed that she prevented mortals from learning about the underworld and the afterlife and prevented them from entering her realm. Her palace, Ganzir, has seven gates and is located near the gates of the land of the dead. Ereshkigal was the sole queen of the underworld until she took the deity Nergal, who became her confidant and consort and helped her rule the underworld.

As feared as she was for her role as the keeper of the dead and the queen of the underworld, Ereshkigal was also highly esteemed and respected by her followers. She's featured in the myth of the Descent of Inanna, which concludes by celebrating Ereshkigal.

Like her sister, Ereshkigal was also associated with dark sensuality, as witnessed by her portrayal as a winged naked woman in ancient terra-cotta plates. The woman carries symbols of all-encompassing power with her wings pointing downward. Standing with two owls on either side, her feet are shaped like talons, and she stands on two lions that lie on top of the mountains. According to other illustrations, Ereshkigal reigned over the vast wilderness of the underworld, which is why she was associated with wild creatures. Besides lions and owls, she is also portrayed holding feathers, snakes, and gemstones like lapis lazuli. However, her illustrations are rare as Mesopotamians only created depictions of something they wanted to bring attention to, which wasn't the case with a goddess they feared.

Being the Queen of the Underworld, it's easy to see why Ereshkigal fits the archetype of the Dark Goddess. She is the perfect embodiment of the journey through and toward the shadow. While she beckoned the departed souls toward her, she could also summon the courage, power, and light one needs to let go of grief and hurt. Those who hear her call or are curious to work with her also claim that Ereshkigal is an excellent source of empowerment during ancestral healing or worship practices.

Ereshkigal encourages everyone to have an open mind and heart, even toward the pain that looking back to the past inevitably brings. She reminds everyone that while meeting their deepest pain is challenging, it doesn't mean they have to look for solutions to dispel this feeling right away. In fact, in these cases, quick fixes don't do any good but can delay the healing process. What they truly need is compassion, love, understanding, and being present in the emotion to process it. Ereshkigal also asserts that when they accept that embracing pain is part of the rebirth process, they reemerge with more clarity. Some claim that when Ereshkigal fully embraced her pain, she experienced this revival, which brought her sister back to life. At the same time, it allowed her to heal after her husband's death as well.

Ereshkigal teaches her followers to nurture the pain in their shadow so they can turn it into a power and ability to share their gifts with the world. Any demon (ill thoughts, emotions, or behaviors) a person projects outwardly is a mirror of the pain they have yet to embrace within.

Holding the key to liberation, Ereshkigal demands that you face all trepidations, one by one, as a means to learn to cope with the uncertainty, despair, and grief that can accompany them. Once this happens, the person is free of pain and everything else they've kept hidden, which blocks them from living life fully.

They've embraced the darkness within themselves and their ability to explore the shadows and face the darkness hidden in them. As a Dark Goddess, Ereshkigal teaches that the fear of what others say when you decide to embrace your shadow and pain holds a much tighter hold on you than the pain itself. The more a person lets in the pain, the easier it becomes to accept that it won't kill them. Even if it seems that you die a thousand deaths while working through the pain, you will be revived and reemerge pain-free in the end.

This Dark Goddess's lessons for embracing pain highlight the importance of reclaiming sovereignty from within. Ereshkigal prompts those willing to learn from her to reclaim their inner darkness with the same reverence with which they would see their positive aspects. By providing the power for self-empowerment, she helps strengthen your relationship with others and with yourself.

# Chapter 5: Slavic Goddesses

Ancient Slavic lore poses a lot of challenges for historians who wish to explore it, as there are no original written records of their deities, rituals, celebrations, tales, or prayers. Most of the knowledge they possess today comes from secondary sources recorded by monks during the Christianization of the region.

The origins of Slavic mythology can be found in Proto-Indo-European times. According to some researchers, these stories could even date back to the Neolithic period. The Slavs of old were split up into local tribes, each with its own mythology, gods, and beliefs. Even the stories and customs of those who lived in the East were similar to those of the Iranians at the time.

Indigenous oral storytelling and religious practices were replaced by Christianity in the late 12th century when Bishop Absalon and his Danish troops invaded the region. His destruction of the statue of Svantevit, the god of war and abundance, marked the end of ancient Slavic paganism.

There are numerous remarkable deities in the Slavic pantheon. However, this chapter will focus on two of the most famous yet highly misunderstood dark female figures in Slavic mythology, Baba Yaga and Marzanna, along with their aspects. Reading this chapter, you will understand the etymology of their names, learn about their characteristics and the accompanying symbolism, explore the roles they play in folklore, and find out about the rituals and celebrations associated with them.

Slavic Goddess.[13]

# Baba Yaga

Baba Yaga is a notorious witch in Slavic folklore.[14]

Originating in Slavic folklore, Baba Yaga is a notorious witch and the ancient deity of old bones who inhabited a mystical den in the vast forest. While she was feared for eating and imprisoning people, especially children, the mythological creature also served as a symbol of female empowerment. According to folklore, the witch also guarded the water of life, which is a powerful liquid that can resurrect the dead.

While Baba Yaga or Jaga is generally understood as the "Grandmother Witch," there is a lot of uncertainty surrounding the true etymology and meaning of the term. "Baba" is a babble word that translates to "old woman." The same word is still used in Bulgaria, Serbia, Croatia, and other nearby countries in the region to refer to "grandmother." Derivatives of the term, which carry mostly negative connotations, are also used in Ukraine and Poland today.

### Etymology

The term "Yaga," however, still raises many questions as it points to no clear etymology. That said, other Slavic languages possess similar sounding vocabulary, such as the terms "jeza," which means "horror" or "anger" in Croatian and Slovenian, and "jedza," which means "witch" in Polish. The oldest mention of Baba Yaga was in 1755 in Mikhail V. Lomonosov's book on Russian Grammar. However, it is generally believed that she existed in the tradition of oral Slavic folklore storytelling long before that. In the book, the grandmother witch was mentioned alongside other Slavic deities. Even though the Slavic gods were mentioned with their equivalents from the Roman pantheon, Baba Yaga appeared without an equivalent.

### Characteristics and Symbolism

Baba Yaga is shown with iron teeth with sharp edges, a very long nose, and long and thin legs of clay. The witch has a thin, bony body and engages in activities that are not conventionally woman-like. This strips away all elements of femininity from her. Instead of flying around on a broom, the witch transports herself in a mortar, rows it with a pestle, and uses the broom to sweep her tracks away.

The mortar and pestle are much more than modes of transportation but are believed to carry strong symbolism. Using these instruments to grind flax, which was then used to spin cloth, was a popular craft among women and was an ironic means of transportation for Baba Yaga, considering that it carried heavy feminine connotations. The mortar and pestle also traditionally symbolize birth, creation, nurture, and death.

Baba Yaga is a very complex and intriguing character. Although she shows up in many tales and plays pivotal roles in them, the old witch's true intentions, motivations, and desires remain unknown. She is helpful yet chaotic and often very vicious, leaving protagonists wishing they hadn't reached out for her help even if they got what they wanted. She is also believed to eat whoever fails to complete her tests and tasks. People can sense Baba Yaga's presence before she appears as she is accompanied by wild winds that cause trees to creak.

Baba Yaga lives in a hut deep in the mystical forest, like most other witches. However, the grandmother witch's hut stands out because it stands on its own pair of enormous chicken legs, allowing it to roam around the forest and search for those who need Baba Yaga's help. The house groans and screams with every move, signifying its terrible state and ominous feel. According to folklore, the hut is a living entity with its own personality.

The hut is surrounded by human bones and skulls. There are human legs and hands for wooden poles and a mouth with sharp teeth for a keyhole. Dangerous, carnivorous dogs guard the hut from intruders. What many people don't know is that Baba Yaga has two sisters, who are also Baba Yagas. In a sense, the Baba Yagas become the archetype of the triple goddess together. The grandmother witch symbolizes death and represents the aspect of the crone in the triple goddess deity archetype, while her sisters represent the aspects of the virgin and the mother.

Baba Yaga possesses unparalleled power as the guardian of the Water of Life and Death. If someone is killed in battle, for instance, Baba Yaga can use the Water of Death to heal all the wounds before using the Water of Life to bring them back to life. In many of the stories in which Baba Yaga appears, a magical oven plays a significant role. The oven has been seen as a symbol of the womb, representing life and birth, since the beginning of time. The oven is also associated with bread, symbolizing the Earth. The Earth is where the body is buried, which is often the step before rebirth or reincarnation, depending on each person's spiritual beliefs.

Despite her viciousness, the witch never goes after people unless they seek her out or provoke her. Most villains in tales and folklore are inherently evil and either feed off cruelty or have lofty motives such as world dominion, while the protagonists are entirely good and have heroic intentions.

On the other hand, Baba Yaga is presented in a neutral light, which is a lot more realistic. The witch doesn't have a moral compass guiding her through life, and her motives are unclear, which is why she doesn't feel the need to engage in either good or evil activities. When someone reaches out to her, she is willing to help them once they prove themselves worthy of her help. If they don't, then she'll do horrible things to them because she has no sense of morality.

### Folklore Features

Baba Yaga often serves as the villain in any tale she's featured in. However, the more you delve into folklore, the more you'll appreciate how she's conveyed as a trickster who evokes change and transformation rather than being a stereotypically evil old crone. Her most famous appearances are in the story *Vasilissa the Beautiful,* where Vasilissa's stepmother sends her to Baba Yaga in search of her fire. On visiting the witch, Vasilissa undergoes a series of tests and quests that she manages to complete. Baba Yaga grants her the fire. However, when Vasilissa returns home, the fire ends up burning and killing her family as a consequence of their cruelty.

She also appears in *The Frog Princess and Baba Yaga,* where a prince marries a frog who he finds out is actually a beautiful woman. However, she ends up leaving him when he betrays her trust. He then goes on a mission to prove himself worthy to her so he can earn her forgiveness. The prince encounters Baba Yaga several times on his quest, who instigates transformations and helps progress the plot.

## Marzanna

Marzanna, the Goddess of Winter and Death.[15]

Marzanna, the Goddess of Winter and Death and the patroness of the underworld, goes by many names like Morana, Marzena, and Morena. Ceres, the Roman goddess of agriculture and fertility, and Hecate, the Greek goddess of witchcraft, necromancy, and night, are Marzanna's equivalents. She is related to Zhiva, the goddess of summer, and Lada, the Spring goddess. She is also Triglav's, the god of war, mother.

One of the most popular folktales regarding the cycle of the seasons is the marriage of Marzanna and Jarylo, the god of spring, war, and agriculture. According to this tale, Marzanna, the daughter of Mokosz, the great mother, and Perun, the god of thunder, was once the goddess of nature. When she was young, Jarylo, who turns out to be her brother, was kidnapped by another deity and taken to the underworld. On his return, neither Marzanna nor Jarylo knew that they were twins. The siblings ended up falling in love and getting married.

Nothing restored balance in the world like their marriage did. Alas, they were the deities of nature and agriculture. However, this peace was short-lived. Marzanna killed Jarylo when he cheated on her, which turned her into the cold, fearful deity of death and nature. Jarylo's death during the fall and the end of their marriage were what initiated the arrival of winter.

Dziewanna, the goddess of spring, and Jarylo then returned to kill Marzanna during the spring, triggering the onset of summer. According to lore, this cycle happens every year, creating the cycle of changing seasons. Neither Jarylo, who symbolizes summer, nor Mazanna, who represents winter, can exist or survive at the same time.

**Etymology**

The name Marzanna is derived from the Proto-Indo-European term "mar," which means death. Many researchers and folklorists believe that the deity is associated with Mars, the Roman deity of war, as his name also evolved from the Latin term "mors," which also translates to death. His name could also be tied to the Russian word "more," which means "pestilence." Marzanna is linked to Mars because the war deity was originally the god of agriculture in the Roman pantheon.

Other folklorists suggest that Marzanna is related to "Mare," an evil spirit found in Slavic and Germanic mythology. Like Marzanna, Mare, too, was thought to create nightmares and accompany sleep paralysis. The Ukrainian term "mara" translates to "dream" and means "hallucinations" in some Slavic languages.

## Characteristics and Symbolism

Researchers suggest that Marzanna is a remnant of broader deity archetypes from regional pantheons, such as the monstrous deity Merihem and Marah, the Canaanite goddess of war. In Slavic mythology, Marzanna is deeply feared as she is believed to attract death. Her appearance also symbolizes the beginning of the winter season. The deity represents the harsh and frigid nature of the season. Her association with both death and the onset of winter symbolizes the end of the natural cycle of humans, the seasons, and agricultural practices.

Winter is also generally representative of dormancy and death, as plants wither, trees lose their leaves, and the overall environment, once vibrant, appears lifeless. In many societies, especially those that rely on agriculture, winter is the most dreaded time of year. People eagerly await spring when the growing season returns.

Before Christianity grew popular in the Slavic region, people were commonly found praying and worshiping Marzanna to bless them with an abundant harvest. There were several rituals and ceremonies dedicated to the deity. They also used symbols like ice, snow, and wooden dolls or ones made of straw and similar natural materials to represent the goddess. Marzanna was thought to die at the end of the winter, also signaling the rebirth of the spring goddess, Lada, and the arrival of spring.

Marzanna sometimes appears in one of her different guises, as Mora, who is the personification of fate. This face of the deity is a malevolent hag who is often regarded as an incarnation of the evil spirit. She leaves her victims breathless and feeds off the blood of men. She is described as a shapeshifting tormentor. She can turn herself into anything, from a large, majestic horse to an unassuming lock of hair.

One tale tells the story of a man who was so repulsed by Marzanna that he ended up fleeing his home. He stormed off on his horse, but little did he know that the deity followed him everywhere he went because she disguised herself as his horse. He eventually grew weary and decided to rest at an inn. When he heard the man groaning at night, the host decided to go into his bedroom. He thought the man was having a nightmare, but he found him being suffocated by a long strand of white hair instead. The host cut the lock in half using a pair of scissors. In the morning, he found the man's white horse dead.

Marui, known as the kitchen demon, is another side of Marzanna. When she senses danger, the deity hides behind the stove of the person who should be alarmed. She twirls around, making scary, thumping noises. She transforms into a butterfly and enters the bedroom, attracting nightmares. Women used to say prayers when they needed to spin something. Otherwise, they believed that the deity would visit at night and ruin all their work.

## Rituals and Celebrations

Slavs who still embrace folk and religious holidays celebrate the arrival of spring with the feast of Maslenitsa. This holiday is also held in commemoration of the dead, encouraging families to come together, join activities like sledding and sleigh rides, and have delicious food and drinks. Pancakes, crepes, cheese, and butter are among the most popular meals that people eat on Maslenitsa, the day before Lent begins, which involves abstaining from consuming dairy products for 40 days.

During the festival, a life-sized figurine of a maiden is made of straw and dressed in rags. The doll, which is a symbolic representation of the goddess Marzanna, is then carried through the fields and either burned or drowned in a body of water. Burning the straw maiden represents the act of getting rid of winter, and drowning the doll signifies the goddess' trip to the underworld.

## Folklore

While the tale of Jarylo and Marzanna perfectly explains the rationale behind the changing seasons, at least two other folklore tales explain the cyclical nature of the seasons. One of these stories revolves around her relationship, as Morana, with Dazbog, the god of the sun, which is very similar to her tale with Jarylo.

Morana and Dazbog were initially lovers and established balance and harmony in the world. However, Dazbog left her for someone else, causing Morana to abandon her duty as the goddess of winter. The days became shorter and warmer, bringing the onset of spring. Morana, however, sought revenge and poisoned Dazbog, and winter returned harsher than it had ever before. Dazbog then banished Morana to the underworld, an event associated with the dormancy of winter. This caused spring, then eventually summer, to return.

Marzanna and the arrival of winter are also associated with the *Enchanted Huntsman* folktale. This tale is very similar to that of Persephone and Demeter, which explains the changing seasons, too. While Persephone, Demeter's daughter (the goddess of agriculture), was out picking flowers, Hades, the god of the underworld, was astounded by her beauty and kidnapped her. Demeter entered a dark state of grief, at which she abandoned her duties, and Earth withered. As a compromise, Hades agreed to send Persephone out from the underworld for a portion of every year. When Persephone comes out, spring and summer occur, and when she's in the underworld, fall and winter overtake the Earth.

Marzanna, in the aspect of Morana, seduced the huntsman, who happened to be the god of the sun. He was charmed by her beauty and fell in love with her. As Hades did to Persephone, Morana trapped the huntsman's soul, which symbolizes light, warmth, and summer, in a magic mirror representing the underworld. This cut the days short and led to the emergence of winter and its harsh weather conditions. According to this lore, spring only arises when Morana's sister Zhiva, the goddess of summer, arrives after Morana's symbolic burning and drowning rituals during Maslenista. This recurrent theme, whether with Jarylo and Marzanna, Persephone and Demeter, Morana and Dazbog, or Morana and the huntsman, shows how people around the world always tried to explain worldly phenomena through common archetypes.

Baba Yaga and Marzanna are two widely feared, dark, and powerful women in Slavic mythology. Reading their mythology, anyone would think that they're inherently evil villains. However, when you learn more about them, you come to learn that they're deeply misunderstood. Both figures open a window into the Slavic culture and show how people at that time and place attempted to make sense of the world around them.

# Chapter 6: Hindu Goddesses

Hindus believe in one supreme god called Brahman. They are also polytheists and believe in the existence of multiple gods and goddesses who reflect aspects of Brahman characteristics.

This chapter provides a comprehensive and insightful exploration of the Hindu Dark Goddesses Kali/Kaalika, Durga, Chinnamasta, and Chamunda.

Hindu Goddesses.[16]

# Kali

Kali is usually depicted with blue skin.[17]

Kali is depicted as a frightening figure with black or blue skin and four arms, wearing a skirt made of arms and a necklace made of skulls, with her tongue sticking out, and she is holding a knife covered in blood.

## Mythology

Kali was the daughter of the war goddess Durga, who was a vicious warrior and a destructive force. Durga had ten arms and carried a weapon in each one. In one battle, she was fighting the buffalo demon, Mahishasura. She arrived riding a lion to frighten her enemies. However, it didn't work, as the demon was invincible. Durga was furious for failing to defeat him. Suddenly, something burst from her forehead. It was Kali, created from her mother's wrath, filled with bloodlust and a destructive nature. She devoured all the demons on the battlefield and wore their heads as a necklace.

However, Kali's violence didn't stop there. She attacked any deity or human who sinned or made a mistake. She was out of control, and neither the gods nor mankind knew what to do with her. Shiva, who was also her husband, had no choice but to intervene. He lay down on her path, and it was only when she stepped on him that she suddenly became ashamed for failing to recognize her husband and was then able to calm down.

In another birth myth, Parvati, the goddess of love, shed her skin and transformed into Kali.

In another version of her birth story, the mighty demon called Daruka was terrorizing mankind and the deities. According to legend, only a woman could kill him. The gods asked Parvati to save them and kill the demon. She transformed into Kali and put an end to Daruka.

In one last myth, a demon called Raktabija was causing trouble on Earth. Even the gods felt helpless and didn't know what to do with him. He was different from any other demon they met because he was able to make new demons with every drop of his blood. So attacking him was impossible.

The gods agreed to work together and create a super-being to defeat Raktabija, and this being was Kali. She devoured all the demons without spilling one drop of blood.

Kali wasn't a thoughtless and merciless murderer. In one myth, a group of thieves kidnapped a monk and were planning to kill him near her statue. Kali was enraged that they dared to harm a monk. Suddenly, her statue came to life, and she punished the thieves.

### Key Characteristics

If you observe these stories, you will notice that Kali is a mother figure. She only killed demons to keep her people safe; she isn't a murderer but a protector.

Although she is recounted in an unattractive manner, she is described in many poems as voluptuous, young, and attractive, with a very nice smile, which many men find irresistible. She is a force of creation and is associated with traits of tantric creativity.

### Popular Forms

- **Dhumavati:** an incarnation of Kali as a widow.
- **Kamala Kali:** goddess of prosperity and wealth.
- **Shodoshi:** a seductress form of Kali.
- **Tara:** known for her violence and blue color.
- **Bhairavi Kali:** a motherly figure and bringer of death.
- **Shamsana Kali:** a more human version of Kali with only two arms and no protruding tongue.

### Symbolism

You probably think that Kali is a heartless murderer. However, the goddess only kills demons. She rarely ever hurts a human being or another deity. In fact, she liberated the souls of many innocent people and helped them to live better lives. Since Kali is also depicted naked, she has become a symbol of sexuality, nurturing, and purity. She is also sometimes shown with three eyes to symbolize omniscience.

Although most of the myths about Kali portray her as bloodthirsty, she is highly venerated and extremely popular among her people mainly because of her role as a tantric goddess. Tantric deities are a pantheon of goddesses who follow the rules and principles of Hinduism.

### Duality

Kali represents the destructive aspect of the dark feminine, tearing down illusions and ego to pave the way for spiritual transformation. Even though she is associated with violence, Kali is a loving mother figure who represents fertility, creativity, and feminine energy. Her duality plays a big role in her symbolism. She is a terrifying figure who could kill mercilessly, yet she also represents the metaphysical affairs associated with death.

Her four arms perfectly reflect her duality. She holds a demon's head and a sword in two hands and blesses her followers with the others.

### Dark Feminine

Kali's appearance is different from any other deity. Her features are fierce and terrifying. She rules over death, doomsday, destruction, and time. She is also the goddess of violence, sexuality, and motherly love. It is believed that Kali is the incarnation of Parvati, the Hindu god Shiva's wife. "Kali" means "she who is death" or "she who is black."

### Archetype

Kali symbolizes protection and love. She connects her worshipers to their emotions, strength, and power. She motivates you to be committed, passionate, and alive. She is the archetype of wild women who are in touch with their instincts and emotions.

### Worship/Rituals

### Instructions:

1. Find a picture of Kali.
2. Sit in a quiet place with no distractions.
3. Light a white candle and take a few deep breaths.

4. Repeat "I am safe and protected" three times.
5. Think of everything that has been upsetting you lately, and focus on them for two to five minutes.
6. Open your eyes and focus on Kali's pictures.
7. Take in every detail and say what you notice either in your mind or out loud.
8. Only focus on Kali and repeat her name out loud for three minutes.
9. Close your eyes and invoke Kali. Ask her energy to flow through you.
10. Spend a few minutes with her, then thank her.

# Durga

Durga is also called Devi or Shakti.[18]

Durga is also called Devi or Shakti. She is the mother of the universe and protector of all mankind and deities. She is one of the most significant and popular goddesses in Hinduism. She represents harmony and everything good in the universe.

## Mythology

The buffalo demon, Mahishasura, was terrorizing the world, and the gods tried to capture him but failed. So Shiva, the Supreme Being, and the destroyer, Brahma, the creator, and Vishnu, the god of preservation, created Durga to kill the demon. She was a beautiful, strong, brave, and fierce warrior. No one could ever defeat her. She was created as a grown woman ready to fight. She fought Mahishasura viciously and slayed him while he was transforming into a buffalo.

Durga fought many demons and protected the world from destruction and bloodshed on multiple occasions. Many of these demons represented negative qualities like anger, arrogance, hypocrisy, pride, and greed. So Durga was also protecting the human soul and fighting evil forces so people would live in harmony with one another.

## Key Characteristics

Durga is a Sanskrit word meaning "fort." Her name reflects her militant and protective nature. She is also called "Durgatinashini," meaning "the one eliminating all sufferings." She is shown as a woman with eight arms, so she is always prepared to fight her enemies from every direction.

She is called Tryambake, meaning "the three-eyed goddess." Her right eye is the sun, and it represents action; her left eye is the moon and symbolizes desire. Her middle eye is fire and represents knowledge.

She is the goddess of strength and war and is illustrated riding a lion and holding weapons.

## Popular Forms

Durga has multiple incarnations:

- Kali
- Bhagvati
- Bhavani
- Ambika
- Lalita
- Gauri
- Kundalini
- Java

Rajeswari When she appeared as herself, she would manifest into any of these nine deities:

- Skandamata
- Kusumanda
- Shailaputri
- Kaalratri
- Brahmacharini
- Maha Gauri
- Katyayani
- Chandraghanta
- Siddhidatri

## Symbolism

Durga has multiple weapons, and each symbolizes an aspect of her personality.

- **Sword:** A symbol of truth and knowledge.
- **Trident:** Healing spiritual, mental, and physical suffering.
- **A budding lotus flower:** Unaccomplished triumph since the battle of good vs. evil is eternal.
- **Thunderbolt:** Strong beliefs in a person's convictions.
- **Bow and arrow:** Her protective abilities and power.
- **Conch shell:** Her connection to the Divine.

## Duality

Dugra may seem more like a destructive weapon than a goddess. However, she has a compassionate side hidden behind her tough and scary exterior. Her only purpose is protecting mankind from the demons who want to bring their downfall.

## Dark Feminine

Durga is a mother goddess with powerful divine femininity. She is creative, nurturing, and protective. Although she is a fierce warrior, she isn't driven by bloodlust. She fights her battles with focus, mastery, and composure. She courageously confronts demons and comes out victorious.

## Archetype

Durga represents the female archetype for one's inner and outer power. She pushes you to set boundaries to protect your energy from negative people.

**Worship/Rituals**
- Offer her flowers to show your devotion.
- Light a candle near her idol.
- Chant "Om Aim Hreem Kleem Chamundaye Vichche" to get rid of bad luck, health problems, and negative energy.

# Chinnamasta

Chinnamasta is a tantric goddess.[19]

Chinnamasta is a tantric goddess. She is an incarnation of the love goddess Parvati. Her name is derived from two Sanskrit words, "Chhinna," meaning severed, and "Masta" meaning head. So the name means "the one with the severed head."

## Mythology

One day, Parvati and her attendants went to take a bath at the Mandakini River. Suddenly, for some mysterious reason, Parvati was aroused, and her color changed to black. At the same time, for unknown reasons, her attendants also got very hungry and demanded to be fed right away. Since she was a motherly figure, she couldn't see them suffering. She made the ultimate sacrifice and severed her head with a sword.

Blood streams were coming out of her neck, which she used to feed her attendants. After they were full, she placed her head back in its place.

Another myth about Chinnamasta's birth is similar to Kali's and Durga's story. There was a war between demons and gods. The gods were outnumbered, and the demons were too strong for them. So they asked the goddess Mahashakti for assistance. She fought the demons and killed them, then she severed her head to drink her blood.

## Key Characteristics

Chinnamasta is depicted holding her severed head in her left hand and a sword in her right hand. In other illustrations, she is depicted with four arms, naked, wearing ornaments and a skull garland. The severed head is usually drinking blood coming out of her neck.

She represents sexual desires, life, death, and self-control, and she is the supreme goddess, the mother of the universe, and the goddess of transformation and feminine energy.

## Popular Forms

- Indrani, goddess of wrath and jealousy
- Bhairavi, goddess of decay
- Varnini, an attendant
- Dhakini, the sky dweller
- Vajravairochani is another name for Chinnamasta
- Chanda Prachandi Devi, the demon destroyer

## Symbolism
- Chinnamasta has a serpent around her neck, which represents power.
- Her naked body is a symbol of worldly things and abandonment.
- Severing her head symbolizes letting go of her ego.
- She is depicted standing over two dead bodies, reflecting her control over her sexual desires.

## Duality
Chinnamasta's scary image is completely different from her caring and compassionate nature. Cutting her head off may seem psychotic to some people, but she did it out of love and devotion to feed her attendants. She only fights demons to protect mankind.

## Dark Feminine
Chinnamasta is a symbol of sacrifice, courage, and feminine power.

## Archetype
Chinnamasta is an archetype of your subconscious, and tapping into it to come up with loving changing ideas.

## Worship/Rituals
Valediction to Chinnamasta

## Instructions:
1. Get a statue of Chinnamasta.
2. Light a scented candle as an offering to the goddess.
3. Ask her for forgiveness, then make an offering and place it at her feet.
4. Fill a conch shell with water.
5. Sprinkle it on yourself to gain her blessings.

# Chamunda

Chamunda is associated with Shiva.[20]

Before Chamunda joined the Hindu pantheon, she was worshiped by different tribes. Chamunda is associated with Shiva. She is the only goddess to emerge from the energy of the supreme goddess since all the gods that came before her were males. She stands out for having a different appearance and weapons.

## Mythology

There were once two demon brothers called Shumbha and Nishumbha. They were extremely ambitious and wanted to take over the world. So they hid in a temple and tortured themselves for thousands of years. Their actions impressed Brahma, the creator, who told them they could have any reward they wanted. They asked that no man nor male god would have any power over them. This made them immortal, as no one could ever hurt or kill them.

They became powerful enough to execute their plan and conquer the world. The gods weren't pleased with the demons' growing power, so the goddess Devi Parvati decided to put an end to them. She resided in a place near the demons, hoping that they or their attendants would notice her. Her plan worked, and because of her exquisite beauty, she caught the attention of one of the attendants.

He told Shumbha about her, and Shumbha asked for her to be brought to his court right away. However, Devi Parvati refused, which angered the demon brothers. They commanded their attendants to bring her by force. They were worried that someone was supporting her and turning her against them.

Their attendants tried for one last time to ask her nicely to join the demons, but she still refused. They were tired of her and decided to kidnap her and take her to Shumbha. When they tried to catch her, she roared at them so loudly they were turned to ashes. She sent her lion after their army of demons, and they devoured them.

Shumbha and Nishumbha were furious and sent a huge army after her, led by demons Chanda and Munda. When Devi Parvati saw the army approaching, Chandika Jayasundara emerged from her forehead and defeated them, killing Chanda and Munda. Devi Parvati then drank their blood and danced to celebrate her victory. She called her Chamunda, a contraction of Chanda and Munda, for her brave and fearless victory.

### Key Characteristics

Chamunda is the goddess of nature, war, famine, and disasters, and she is the chief yogini, a group of Tantric gods who act as devi Pavarti attendants. She is portrayed as having three eyes, four arms, red skin, and thick red hair decorated with a crescent moon and skulls.

### Popular Forms

Chamunda has eight different forms. She is one of the Saptamatrikas, seven mother goddesses.

### Symbolism

Chamunda's fierce features reflect her strength and power against her enemies and how she protects her worshipers from evil. The skull necklace represents life's cycle, which ends in death.

### Duality

Chamunda may be one of the most frightening deities in Hinduism, but she is compassionate, loving, a mother figure, and a protector to all her worshipers. People pray to her to protect them, fight demons and evil powers, and to also provide guidance and strength.

### Dark Feminine

Chamunda is the female energy of the god of death, Yama. She is a terrifying figure who brings famine, disasters, and epidemics.

### Archetype

Chamunda's archetype is also the subconscious mind, as she helps you tap into this part of yourself to discover who you truly are.

### Worship/Rituals

**Instructions:**

1. Find a room with no distractions.
2. Place crystals like rose quartz and citrine on the floor to make a circle.
3. Sit in a comfortable position in the circle.
4. Call on your ancestors, spirit guides, or guardian angels for assistance.
5. Take five long and deep breaths.
6. Make an offering to the goddess, like wine.
7. Focus on what you are feeling right now.
8. Set an intention to let go of anything holding you back, either by thinking about it or by chanting, "Let it go."
9. Repeat Chamunda's mantra on a bead: "Om Eim Hrim Kilm Chamundayei Vechei Namaha," meaning "Om and salutations to the radiant one who has wisdom and power."
10. Lie down and take a few deep breaths so you can absorb the energy.
11. Express your gratitude to Chamunda and all the spirits who assisted you in your ritual.

Looking at the pictures of any of these Hindu goddesses can give you nightmares. However, you shouldn't judge them by their appearance. They can be killers, and sometimes their anger gets out of control, but they never harm a human being, and their instinct is to always protect.

They are all mother figures who were willing to do anything to keep their children (worshipers) safe.

Remember to be respectful when you call on them and express your gratitude after every ritual. You don't want to get on their bad side. Live by the morals they represent and be kind, caring, and compassionate. Don't be in a rush to establish a connection with them, and understand that these things take time.

# Chapter 7: African Goddesses

Many people are familiar with Norse, Greek, and ancient Egyptian mythologies. Their gods and goddesses are usually featured in movies, TV shows, and literature. Who doesn't know the Norse God Thor, the Greek Goddess Aphrodite, or the Egyptian Goddess Cleopatra? However, there is an equally fascinating and enchanting mythology that doesn't get the same attention: ancient African mythology. Many gods and goddesses in Africa deserve the same recognition as their Western counterparts.

This chapter focuses on the Dark Goddesses in African mythology.

African Goddess.[31]

# Oya

Oya, the goddess of magic and graveyards.[22]

Oya is a goddess worshiped in many African traditions, such as Yoruba and Santeria. However, she isn't usually referred to as a goddess but as an Orisha. This is a term that describes supernatural beings or deities that help mankind and act as intermediaries between them and the supreme god, Oldumare.

Oya is a fierce goddess who rules over the winds and storms. She can either bring a gentle breeze on a hot summer day or a hurricane destroying everything in her way. However, Oya has a much darker side as the guardian of the cemeteries and the dead. She watches over graveyards and protects the spirits. She exists in the realm of the living and the dead and can easily travel between both worlds. Oya shares a unique bond with the spirits of the departed, and she accompanies them to the other world where they will spend their eternity.

### Origin

Oya originates from the African religion Yoruba. Her name is derived from the African phrase "O Ya," meaning "she tore," which refers to her explosive nature. She is the daughter of Obatala, the Orisha of mankind and compassion, and Yemaya, the mother of all Orishas.

## Mythology

In Yoruba mythology, Oya was a human being who had great powers. She was a fierce warrior who protected the weak, especially women. She also liberated many enslaved people in the Yoruba revolution. Since Oya didn't live an ordinary life, she was gifted with an extraordinary destiny after she died and became an Orisha.

She was married to the Orisha of thunder, Shango. He was also married to two other Orishas, Oba and Oshun, who were also Oya's sisters. Interestingly, Shango was also their brother. Oya was his favorite wife, and they had a passionate relationship. They were madly in love and one of the strongest couple deities in Yoruba.

Sadly, Oya didn't have any children sired by her husband. She got pregnant nine times, but none of her children survived birth. She kept their memory alive by wearing nine-colored scarves around her waist. In another legend, she made a sacrifice by offering a sacred piece of cloth, and she was blessed with four sets of twins and a ninth child. For this reason, she is called "The mother of nine."

## Attributes

Oya is a brave, courageous, and powerful warrior. She is shown as a beautiful and strong black woman carrying a sword in one hand to bring change and cut through any obstacles her followers may face. On the other hand, she is holding a fan to control storms and winds.

Oya is associated with destruction, transformation, and change. She can control earthquakes, tornadoes, winds, storms, and lighting. She is also the Orisha of clairvoyance, intuition, and rebirth. She is very wise, and women call on her when facing a conflict they can't resolve on their own.

People love and fear Oya. She is a fierce protector and a loving mother to all her followers. However, when she gets angry, she destroys homes and lands, bringing much suffering to her people. She appreciates honesty and justice and can't tolerate lies and deceit.

Oya can also heal. People call on her when their life is out of balance or after the death of a loved one. She is also the goddess of fertility and protector of crops.

Oya has a very famous dance that can either bring gentle wind or violence and chaos. It depends on her mood.

She also rules over the marketplace and keeps her eyes open for con artists and thieves. Merchants and traders usually pray to her before they embark on a business endeavor.

### Cultural Significance

Although Oya originated in the Yoruba religion, her cultural significance extends to other cultures and traditions. In the Brazilian Candomblé, Oya represents compassion, and she is the protector of all women. In the Cuban religion, Santeria, she represents the modern woman who defies social norms. This shows that Oya is a universal Orisha who embodies various aspects that resonate with people from different cultures.

Oya's cultural significance is shown in literature, music, and art. For instance, she was featured in Nigerian writer Chinua Achebe's poems.

### Symbols

In one African legend, Oya had a black ram who was a loyal and trusted friend. However, he turned against her and tried to kill her. She was heartbroken over this betrayal and swore to never trust a ram again. Since then, female goats have become one of her symbols.

Other symbols:

- Iruke
- Machete
- Marketplace
- Cemetery
- Fire
- Thunderbolt
- Wind
- Niger River
- Number nine
- Guinea hen
- Buffalo

- Plums
- Amber
- Violet
- Musk
- Dark chocolate
- Ruby
- Moonstone
- Amber
- Burgundy
- Purple
- Brown

### Oya, the Dark Goddess

As the Orisha of new life and rebirth, Oya is considered a Dark Goddess because of her association with death and cemeteries. She guides people away from the darkness and into the light, giving them hope after turmoil. Oya travels between the realms of the living and the dead. She has the power of life and death. She can keep the dead on Earth if they have unfinished business. She can also bring the dead to her whenever she wants. This is why she is called the "Great Mother of Witches (Elders of the Night)."

After a person dies, Oya must take their spirit immediately to the afterlife to keep both realms in order and prevent the dead from roaming around aimlessly among the living. In a way, she protects the living as well from the fear of watching spirits walking around them.

### Rituals/Worship

Worshiping any goddess requires making offerings. Oya loves eggplants, plums, female goat meat, guinea hen meat, pigeon meat, black hen meat, dark chocolate, and red wine.

You can also pray to her when you are experiencing change. If your life is turning upside down, ask Oya to bless you with stability and reassurance. She can take away the negative energy that is disturbing your life.

If you want to communicate with your ancestors, call on Oya. Since she stands between the realm of the living and the realm of the dead, she can deliver your messages to your loved ones.

If you or someone requires healing, hold an egg and pray to Oya to remove the negative energy making them sick. Then, crack the egg in a glass of water to release the negativity.

If Oya is calling on you, she will bring sudden changes in your life to push you toward growth and transformation. She may also appear to you in dreams or send you one of her symbols, like storms or lighting. She is trying to communicate with you if you find yourself drawn toward her mythology or symbols.

### Invoking Oya:

1. Set up an altar during a wind, lightning, rain, or storm.
2. Add any of her symbols or her picture to the altar.
3. Light a purple or any dark-colored candles.
4. Make an offering.
5. Write your intention on a piece of paper.
6. Sit near the altar in a comfortable position and close your eyes.
7. Clear your mind and focus on your breathing.
8. Visualize Oya and ask for her guidance or to communicate with a departed loved one.

9. Pay attention to what you may see or feel during the meditation.
10. After you finish, express your gratitude to her.

# Yewa

Yewa is one of the most mysterious Orishas. She is Oya's sister and lives with her in graveyards among the dead. She also rules over cemeteries and prevents the spirits from roaming among the living. She is the Orisha of death, loneliness, chastity, virgins, and fertility. However, she doesn't cause death. She just helps the spirits reach their final resting place. She receives the spirits of the dead and takes them to Oya, who escorts them to the afterlife.

## Origins

Yewa originated from the Yoruba religion. Her name is derived from the words "Yeye," meaning mother, and "Awa," meaning our, so she is often referred to as "Our mother." She used to be a patron for women and mothers. Her story is unclear. In one version, she was never a mother because she was never married and was a virgin. She did, however, become the protector and goddess of all virgins.

## Mythology

Yewa wasn't always a dark Orisha who lived in the graves. Her life was completely different. She was a young and naive virgin who was known for her beauty and chastity. Every male Orisha had eyes on her and wanted to possess her. One of these Orishas was Shango, a famous womanizer who seduced many female Orishas. When he saw Yewa, he became infatuated with her and started chasing her.

He seduced her, and the innocent girl had no idea of Shango's intentions. She got pregnant and hoped he would be by her side and support her. However, he disappeared, leaving her all alone. Yewa was humiliated and felt used, desperate, and scared. She then lost her child and buried it under a tree. This experience left her traumatized, and she retreated to the cemeteries to live with her sister.

When Olokun, the Orisha at the bottom of the ocean, learned about what happened to her, he went to the tree and brought back her unborn child to life. He named him Borosia, and he became Olokun's guard.

The rest of the story remains unclear. In one version, she married Boromu, the Orisha of the desert and guardian of the cemetery and human bones. Boromu was in love with her, but he may also have wanted to protect her honor. In another version, she continued living in the cemetery.

There is another less tragic version of Yewa's story. Yewa took a vow of chastity and hid away from temptation in her father's Obatala castle. When Shango heard about the beautiful virgin, he decided he must have her. When he reached the castle and saw her, he was mesmerized by her beauty. Yewa also felt a strong attraction to Shango, and her feelings confused and scared her.

She went to her father and sought his guidance. Obatala loved his daughter, but he understood that she must be protected from these lustful feelings. So he sent her to the realm of the dead to guard over the cemeteries. No man or Orisha could ever come close to that realm, so no one could tempt or distract her from her vow.

### Attributes

Yewa is depicted as a beautiful and skinny woman dressed in pink who can transform into an owl. She was originally a water spirit, but she then became a virgin goddess of decorum, reclusiveness, and morality. She is a guardian of the innocent, but if you disrespect her, she will bring suffering and pain.

She is extremely diligent, wise, intelligent, strong-willed, sweet, and knowledgeable. Yewa is a mother figure and an archetype of chastity. Orula, the Orisha of oracles and wisdom, bestowed on her the power of clairvoyance. Yewa rules over the cosmos and the night skies. She can transform water into gas to create clouds and rain. She is associated with the darkness, where spirits find themselves after they leave their human form.

### Cultural Significance

Yewa originated in Nigeria. She is highly revered in Africa and was the Orisha of the Yewa River. In Yoruba, Candomblé, and Santeria, Yewa is the Orisha of death. She was first an Orisha of birth, fertility, and water. Then, she became responsible for separating the realm of the dead from the living. This change took place during the slave trade. When enslaved people arrived in South America, they established a religion derived from Yoruba called Santeria, where Yewa was the Orisha of death. After her marriage to Boromu, she became associated with death like her husband.

In Cuba, she is also the Orisha of death and rules over the cemeteries, and she also represents purity and virginity.

## Symbols
- Any body of water like ponds, lakes, or rivers.
- Pink veils
- Gravestones
- Fridays
- Owls
- Seashells
- Dolphins
- Fish
- White lotus (represents innocence and purity.)
- Meadowsweet flowers
- Orchids
- Chrysanthemums
- Lilies
- Flowers
- Scents like apricot, water lily, bergamot, vanilla, rose, orange, and mint.
- Pearls
- Pink
- Number 11

## Yewa, the Dark Goddess

Yewa is the guardian of the graveyards. She dances over people's tombs to bring peace to their souls and let them know she is here guarding and protecting them. However, she still protects the innocent, pure, and virgins. If someone tries to harm them, she makes them suffer.

Yewa believes that the dead should be respected. So if someone mocks them or desecrates their graves, she will bring her wrath down on them.

## Rituals/Worship

To properly worship Yewa and avoid her wrath, never swear in front of her altar or image. Since she is a virgin, refrain from offending her by talking about sex, having sex, or making sexual innuendos near her altar. Respect all people and never start a fight with anyone.

If Yewa is calling you, you will experience spiritual purity and a desire to be alone. You will also be more interested in introspection or meditation. Yewa may also come to you in dreams, either as herself or sending you one of her symbols like a cemetery or a skull.

Make offerings to Yewa such as white guinea fowl meat, white pigeon meat, white hen meat, goat meat, and herbs like fennel, cypress, and tua.

**Invoking Yewa:**
1. Find a quiet place.
2. Build an altar and add any symbols of her or her pictures.
3. Light black or burgundy candles.
4. Make an offering like flowers or fish.
5. Write down your intention on a piece of paper, then place it on the altar.
6. Sit in a comfortable position and close your eyes.
7. Take a few deep breaths.
8. Visualize Yewa and ask for her guidance.
9. Express your gratitude after you have finished.

# Ala

Ala is a goddess from the Odinala tradition that originated in South Nigeria. Odinala holds women in very high regard and even puts them ahead of men. Ala is called "The mother of all things," and she is present at the beginning and end of one's life.

## Origins

Ala is an Igbo word meaning "ground." Her mother is the goddess of fertility for animals and humans, guardian of the harvest, ruler of the underworld, and the goddess of the earth, and her father is the great god Chuku.

## Mythology

In Ibo regions, Ala is worshiped in square-shaped homes called "Mbari." Inside, there are large, bright-colored statues of Ala. She usually sends a bee nest or a snake to the location where she wants her followers to build a Mbari. Men and women who help build this sacred structure feel honored and connected to the goddess.

### Attributes

She is the goddess of death, cleansing, joy, luck, creativity, and morality. She is the Earth mother, guardian of fertility, ruler of the underworld, and guardian of the harvest.

She has the power to make a child grow in their mother's womb. After birth, she stays with the child to guide and protect them until they reach adulthood. She also represents the four seasons.

Ala teaches people how to live honestly by emphasizing values like honor and loyalty. She is associated with morality, makes laws for the Igbo people to live by, and judges their actions. These laws are called Omenala, and if one breaks them, it is a great insult to Ala.

She is usually depicted carrying a small child since she is the protector of children and women.

### Cultural Significance.

Ala is highly revered among the Igbo people. She is one of their main deities, and they live by her rules.

### Symbols

- Yams
- Crescent moon
- Ants
- Python

### Ala, the Dark Goddess

She is the underworld queen, and when a person dies, she takes their spirit into her womb so they can rest in peace. She has an army of ants to punish those who break her laws. They first appear in nightmares as a warning so you can make things right. Her army will bring severe punishment and suffering if you don't return to the right path.

### Rituals/Worship

There are different ways to worship Ala. Light a candle when you wake up every morning to welcome her. You can also make an offering of yam since it is her favorite food.

The best time to worship Ala is during the spring. Build an altar, add her pictures and symbols, and light a candle.

African Dark Goddesses are strong and fierce and must be respected. Although they have dark aspects, they keep the realm of the living safe and in order by taking the souls of the dead to the afterlife. They care about the spirits either by keeping them safe like Ala, who keeps them in her womb, or by keeping them company like Yewa, who dances on their graves.

They also serve the living by providing guidance and taking them from the darkness to the light. Always appease the Dark Goddess because they have a bad temper.

# Chapter 8: Celtic/Irish Goddesses

People often hear the terms Celtic and Irish Mythology used interchangeably, begging the question of whether or not they are one and the same. The answer is **no**.

Irish mythology is similar to Celtic mythology, like *Protestantism* is to *Christianity*, one branch of a big tree. The pre-Christian beliefs of the Celtics housed the tales of the Scots, Irish, and Brittonics. Olden myths and rituals were passed down the generations through word of mouth. Of the three main branches, the Irish stories are the best preserved, thanks to the efforts made by the Christian monks who wove the tales into the historical records during the Middle Ages.

In most theologies, ancient deities were patrons for more than one realm and were seen as protectors of acts like love, fertility, and land. Often, they shared the responsibilities of the realms with other gods, making it hard to distinguish the specific roles of each one of them.

The Celtic and Irish mythologies have an enigmatic ambiance to them. Home to many magical and other-worldly beings whose tales can keep you on the edge of your seat.

As you make your way through the chapter, you'll find yourself engrossed in the world of the dark and powerful deities that the ancestors revered and feared at the same time.

Celtic Goddess.[38]

# The Morrigan

She is one of the most prominent and fierce figures in Celtic History; a formidable warrior, unchallenged by anyone, avidly worshiped despite her ferociousness, beauty, and brutality.

### Who Is She?

The great queen goddess represented war, fate, and death. She was also a gifted shapeshifter, with her most common transformation being into a raven. She would often appear before battles in her raven form, either terrifying or inspiring the soldiers to fight harder. In some other tales, she would appear as a wolf or an eel. She sometimes employed her shapeshifting skills to transform into a beautiful woman so she could seduce powerful men. More tales show the goddess depicted as an old ugly hag.

Her name often changed with whomever was telling the story. She was referred to as the Celtic goddess of death, Morrigu, or the queen of the triple goddesses, among many other names.

Her name is a subject of controversy among scholars. Some say that the first part of her name, "Mor," is interpreted in old Irish as the word phantom. Others are convinced that it is linked to the Anglo-Saxon word "maere," which translates to nightmare or death. At times, people spelled the word "Mor" with an accent on the O, turning its meaning into great.

The other half of her name, "Rigan," means queen and corresponds with the Latin word Regina, meaning great queen. Put together, you've got "great queen" or "Phantom Queen" to add to the list of names she had.

In the old scriptures, it was assumed that she could foresee the death of warriors in battle, often influencing the outcome of the conflict.

In some Irish tales, she was addressed as one of the three war goddesses, along with her other two sisters, Macha and Neman or (Badb). In others, she was represented as both an individual and three distinct personalities under a single name. Those tales sometimes referred to Macha, Badb, and Neman as the Morrigan. Other tales are named Danu or Anand instead of Neman. These discrepancies cast a shadow on the truth of how the goddess was seen through the eyes of the ancient Celtics. When she's viewed as three goddesses the Morrigan gains more powers than when she stands alone. On her own, she is the great goddess of war and death, while with her sisters, she becomes the guardian of land, goddess of fertility, and a sovereignty goddess.

The Morrigan can easily be compared with the Norse Valkyries, the Furies, and Kali of Hindu mythology, goddess of destruction and transformation. So, in a nutshell, the Morrigan is heavily linked to carnage, war, and blood.

**Her Symbols**

The Morrigan is associated with more than one symbol in the Celtic/Irish Mythology. The symbol would change depending on the version of the story being told and the perspective from which it's recited.

**1. Ravens**

In most stories, at the mention of a raven, thoughts immediately go to death and the end of life since the birds are often seen after battles picking at the remains of the dead. They also symbolized witchcraft and magic, which is a common association even today. Since the goddess often chose to take the form of the raven, specifically in battle, it made sense that it would be one of her symbols.

## 2. The Moon

This representation has something to do with the goddess having a triple nature. The ancestors considered the moon's changing phases between waxing, waning, and full as a heavenly cycle. Also, as it continuously changes its shape throughout the month, it reminds the people of the goddess' ability to shapeshift herself.

## 3. The Triskelion

In the old days, this symbol was considered one of the main signs of divinity, coincidentally also signifying the number three. It made sense to attribute it to the Morrigan since she was made up of three goddesses in some beliefs.

## The Family Tree

In Irish folklore, the goddess is said to be one of the three daughters (a variation of those sisters was Badb, Anann, and Macha) of the Irish goddess and sorceress Ernmas. It was said that she was the wife of the god Dagda. There are two versions about her origin and when exactly she came to be. The Tuatha de Danann places the mother and daughter with the tribe of supernatural and mythical beings and associates them with the goddess Danu. In this version of the tale, the Morrigan is believed to have fought alongside her sisters in the battle against the Fomorions and the Firbolg, using magic to win the fight and gain a foothold in Ireland.

In the Ulster Cycle, which some believe precedes the Tuatha de Danann, the Morrigan is said to have existed in the copper age in 3000 BCE. However, not much evidence supports this theory. In her early depictions in Irish literature, she was referred to as "Monster in the form of a Woman" and "Ominous Creature," which gives you an idea of why she was consistently linked to death.

Her role in death consisted of prophesying and influencing it at times. Her other two sisters completed the cycle, with each one representing a different characteristic of the relationship between life and death.

## The Morrigan and Cu Chulainn

One of the well-known stories of the Morrigan involves the Celtic Hero Cu Chulainn. It is said that the warrior was following a stray heifer that he'd lost. In his mind, the heifer had been stolen and placed in another location. He found it in the same territory where the Morrigan happened to be at the same time.

The young man started attacking the Morrigan with sharp language, accusing her of the theft without knowing that he was in the presence of a deity. The goddess then turned herself into a raven and landed on a branch near him. The warrior immediately backtracked and asked for forgiveness, for he would have never disrespected the goddess had he known who she was. The Morrigan then proceeded to accuse him of touching her in his rage, which infuriated the warrior, sending him into another offensive tirade at the goddess. Instead of exacting divine vengeance then and there, the Morrigan warned the warrior that he would die in the coming battle, and she would be there to witness his demise.

The day of battle came. The warrior was in a fight with Queen Maeve (also known as Med), attempting to defend the province of Ulster from her invasion. Out of nowhere, a fair maiden happened upon him. The beautiful woman offered herself to the hero but was promptly rejected. The young beauty turned out to be the Morrigan. Furious at the way she had been treated, she turned herself into an eel and attempted to attack Cu Chulainn as he was crossing a fjord. The young warrior fought back and injured the animal.

Adamant to restore her wounded pride, the goddess then changed into a wolf and went after the hero, charging a herd of cattle in an attempt to trample him under their feet. Cu Chulainn then used his slingshot to aim at the beast's eye, firing a stone and temporarily blinding the predator.

The goddess was not one to admit defeat, and she then changed form into a cow. In that form, she was able to inflame the rest of the herd, urging them to stampede toward the warrior.

The brave and cunning warrior managed to evade the herd and shoot yet another stone at the goddess's leg, breaking it immediately and forcing her to retreat.

After triumphing in battle against both Queen Maeve and the Morrigan, Cu Chulainn made his way back to his base, exhausted, seeking company and refuge. Along the way back, he met an old woman milking a cow. The warrior was too tired to notice that the old hag had similar injuries to the ones he had inflicted on the animals who attacked him. A blind eye and an injured leg.

Unable to assess the situation properly, Cu Chulainn stopped to chat with the old woman, who offered him milk to quench his thirst. The young man accepted the gesture, drank the milk, and blessed the old woman for her kindness. Upon doing so, unbeknownst to him, he restored the mighty goddess to her full strength.

The goddess was satisfied with her trickery of the warrior and did not attempt to engage in another fight with him.

It is said that the pair met once again before another one of Cu Chulainn's battles. On his way to the fight, he came upon a woman scrubbing blood off a suit of armor, which was considered a dark omen to see before a battle. He passed the woman and continued on his way. During the battle, he was fatally wounded. Using what was left of his strength, he tied himself to a boulder in an upright position to frighten any further oncoming enemies. A crow then settled on his shoulder, and he went into a deep sleep, never to wake again.

## Macha

Macha is renowned for her powerful magic and need for vengeance.[14]

One of the goddesses thought to be a part of the Morrigan in certain myths is Macha. On the other hand, she was an individual member of the Tuatha de Danann, renowned for her powerful magic and voracious need for vengeance. She was rumored to have lived in Emain Macha's old fort.

She was the goddess of kinship, fire, fertility, land, horses, and warfare. Like the Morrigan, Macha was seen as a death omen who materialized as an apparition to warn people of impending doom.

Macha was revered as the big Mother Earth, the ultimate female, and the murderer of men. She was also known by several other names, such as Dana and Badb (crow or raven). Her name translated to "field" or "land plain." She was closely linked to the images of crows, acorns, and horses. Her three main attributes were her sexual fertility, her rural upbringing, and her maternal reproductive ability.

Macha is best known through five famous tales:

### 1. Partholon's Daughter

In the Leabhar Gabhala, she is referred to as the daughter of Partholon. In ancient legend, the Patholonians were among the second wave of settlers that came to Ireland. Some claim they were descendants of Noah. However, it is believed that they succumbed to a plague. Her reference in this tale is not prominent, and some believe that she was only included as an attempt by Christian monks to Christianize her.

### 2. Member of the Tuatha De Danann

In this tale, like her sister, the Morrigan, Macha is the daughter of Ernmas and Delbeath. She is depicted as the goddess of battle and war who used her magic to bring forth rain, fog, blood, and fire upon her enemies. It is believed that she may have fallen alongside King Nuada at the hands of Balor of the Baleful Eye at the battle of Moytura.

### 3. Nemed's Wife

In another tale, it is stated that she came along with the third wave of settlers to Ireland with her husband, Nemed. In this story, she doesn't last long, for she dies while cleaning out the land to plant it. She is portrayed as the goddess of fertility and land. Her grave is thought to be in a place called Ard Mhacha (meaning Macha's Height), known today as Armagh.

### 4. Wife of Cruinniuc

In the Ulster Cycle, she is seen as a fairy woman married to a wealthy farmer, Cruinniuc. She bears two children, twins. Macha had warned her husband not to mention her to anyone. During a festival held by the king of Ulster, attended by her husband, he overheard the king bragging about his horses and how fast they were. Unable to contain himself, Cruinniuc declared to the king that his wife could easily outrun any of his horses. Enraged by the insolence of the farmer, the king commanded him to bring forth his wife.

At the time, Macha was in labor and pleaded that the race be postponed. However, the king insisted, and she raced anyway. Macha succeeded in winning the race but at a high cost. She fell to the ground at the finish line, giving birth to her babies. Overcome with pain and anger, she cursed the men of Ulster, condemning them to suffer nine days of labor pain at the time of their greatest need and peril. The curse was to last for nine generations. As her children were brought to life, she was taken from it.

### 5. Macha of the Red Hair (Macha Mhongruadh)

Historians state that in this story, she is believed to have been the daughter of King Aodh Ruadh. The king was known to take turns ruling Ireland with two other kings. Each king was to rule for seven years. After the king's death following his third round, Macha demanded to take his place in the cycle as dictated by her birthright. Needless to say, the other two kings (Díthorba and Cimbáeth) had no interest in ruling with a woman.

They went into battle over the throne, and Macha was victorious, killing Dithorba in the process. After her seven years of ruling concluded, she was challenged by Dithorba's five sons. Macha informed them that she would allow them to battle for sovereignty. They accepted the challenge, and once again, she won. The five sons fled into the wild, and Macha married Cimbaeth to cement her claim to the throne so they could rule together.

The goddess then pursued the five sons alone, disguising herself in the form of a leper. One by one, she seduced and captured them. She then brought them home and forced them to build the fort of Emain Macha.

She ruled the land by her husband's side for seven years until he died, and then she continued to rule for another fourteen by herself until she was killed by Rechtaid Rigderg.

# Badb

Badb is one of the goddesses believed to make up the triad of the Morrigan. She was known in the old days as the battle crow. It was common knowledge among worshipers that she played a role in gathering the souls of the fallen in battle and escorting them into the afterlife.

One of the forms she took was that of a petrifying woman who spreads fear and chaos. The goddess was linked to war, transformation, and a dominating presence that was awe-inspiring to mortals.

Her symbolism included the colors red and white (red clothes and white hair), which represent death in Celtic folklore. She was seen mostly as an old woman with one eye closed, standing on one foot, indicating the connection between the world of the living and the hereafter. She was also represented by crows and wolves, which symbolized guidance and transformation.

### The Cauldron of Rebirth

Her name translates to "the one who boils," as she is seen in some illustrations tending to a magical cauldron in the other world. It was believed that when a warrior died in battle, they would see the goddess in the form of an old, kind woman stirring a cauldron. On meeting the goddess, the deceased warrior is asked whether they wish to stay or be reborn. If they chose to be reborn, they were then required to climb into the cauldron, where the goddess would examine the water within to see what form they would come back as a baby human or an animal with cubs.

The goddess's symbols included the crow, protection, prophecy, and strategy.

### The Battle of Magh Tuired

Badb made a strong appearance in the first and second battles of Magh Tuired. It was said that she appeared on the battlefield alongside her sisters in the form of a terrifying crow. She worked with her sisters to inspire terror in the hearts of their enemies, creating confusion with horrible prophecies they screamed together in the face of their foes. Her fierce cries echoed in the battle, foretelling the defeat of their rivals and the ominous end of the opposing army of Fomorians. These tactics were quite effective in driving the enemy back into the sea.

In another tale, it was said that after she left the battlefields, she would watch over families, becoming a faery (banshee) whose wail signaled the death of a family member.

### The Prophetess

This is the story of the goddess who encountered King Cormac. The king, in need of a place to retire between battles, settles on a hostel owned by a man called Da Choca. As he rests with his soldiers, they notice an old woman washing bloodied clothes at the river. Intrigued, they questioned her, wanting to know what she was up to.

The crone then answers that she is washing the clothes of a king who will soon meet his demise. She appeared again to them in the hostel the same night, white-haired and dressed in red, instilling fear and a sense of horror in their hearts. On the same night, the king's enemies, the Connachta, invaded the hostel and murdered him, fulfilling the goddess's prophecy.

## The Cailleach

Cailleach is associated with seasons and weather.[25]

The Cailleach was associated more with seasons and weather rather than war and destruction. However, the season she was mostly connected to was winter, which in a lot of cultures is considered the withering season. She was known as the goddess of the cold and wind. She was said to be able to determine the length and harshness of winter.

The name of the goddess Caillech means the veiled one. Other opinions suggest that it is the root of other words that describe women, like "cailin," meaning girl.

Cailleach's influence is not limited to Ireland. Her presence was known in Scotland and the Isle of Man as well. She often appears as a veiled old hag with pale and blue skin. Her teeth were red, and she wore clothes decorated with skulls. She could leap across high mountains and ride storms.

Like most of the other deities, the Cailleach had the ability to shapeshift, taking on the form of a huge bird. The veiled goddess was also referred to as a creator deity. She was said to have been responsible for the shaping of the landscape. The tools she used for creation included a hammer she used to control thunder and storms (a close likeness to Thor of Asgard, the Norse God). In other tales, it said that she could control a well that would often overflow and flood the lands.

Stories often connected her with the cycle of life, fertility, death, and rebirth.

No one seemed to agree on whether or not this goddess was good or evil. It all depended on the tale and the narrator. She had a great love for wild and domesticated animals, specifically wolves (if you haven't noticed, there is a common theme regarding wolves among the Celts).

The Cailleach's presence is felt more in Irish and Scottish mythology, with little to no mention in Wales.

**The Age of Cailleach**

The story tells of a wandering friar and his scribe happening upon an old woman's house one day. The friar was curious about her age, to which she replied that she did not know exactly how long she'd been alive. However, she said she slaughtered an ox and made soup out of its bones every year. She told the friar that if he still wished to know her age, he was free to go into the attic and count the bones of the oxen left there.

The scribe climbed up the stairs and started throwing the bones to the friar so he could count. The friar kept note of the number of bones until he ran out of paper, and the pile of bones grew before him. The friar called to the scribe, who then told him that he hadn't even removed the pile from one corner of the attic, which indicated that Cailleach was a great age.

## Cailleach's Influence on the Seasons

There was a seasonal division between Cailleach and Brigid. One ruled the winter and the other spring. In Scottish mythology, Cailleach transforms into Brigid with the coming of spring and then transforms back in winter.

Winter is heralded by the goddess, who rides a wolf and taps her magical staff on the Earth, turning it into ice.

Cailleach would go to the well of youth, drink, and change from a gloomy and chilly winter into a stunning young lady when she was through. The change was the signal for the arrival of spring. This telling of the story encouraged many to believe that they were truly two parts of the same being, Brigid and the spring goddess, rather than two distinct entities.

In the tales that suggested that they were two different entities, Cailleach was believed to turn to stone at the end of winter, discarding her staff beneath a horse or a holly bush.

Because of the harsh nature of winter, the goddess was also linked to death. It was believed that she was responsible for gathering the souls of the departed. She would ride through the skies with the Wild Hunt during the winter solstice.

# Chapter 9: Norse Goddesses

*"Lo there do I see my Father; Lo there do I see my Mother, my sisters, and my brothers; Lo there do I see the line of my people, back to the beginning. Lo, they do call me, they bid me take my place among them, in the halls of Valhalla, where the brave may live forever."*

Movie lovers would recognize this quote as the prayer recited by the Norse Vikings prior to the final battle in the historical masterpiece "The 13th Warrior". It didn't matter that the prayer was made up or historically unverified. The words summed up the lifestyle and beliefs by which the Norsemen led their lives. Their undying faith in their Gods. The high stature of warriors who die in battles and the spoils that await them on the other side.

In recent years, Norse mythology has gained a lot of traction due to the repeated and diverse portrayal of its stories in mainstream media. These stories presented the ancient characters as modern-day heroes.

**Norse Goddess.**[36]

Those who followed the pagan religion and remained immersed in the mythical tales following the emergence of Christianity were often referred to as heathens, a word derived from heaths, meaning the people who lived elsewhere in the countryside.

As you dive into the original stories that inspired these adaptations, you'll be faced with the conundrum of not being able to separate the light from the dark. It is a characteristic of the enthralling tales of the Nordic people that nothing was pure evil or pure good but a realistic mixture of both if you disregard the magic and powers.

Within this chapter, you'll find yourself swaying on the line between the peaks and valleys of morality as it explores the mighty goddesses of Asgard.

# Hel

Hel is the patron of the dead and the underworld.[17]

She is the goddess whose namesake is the same as the place she ruled. Hel, also known as Hela, is the patron of the dead and the underworld. She also assumed the role of guardian of the souls who pass down Helvegr, the road of the dead.

The goddess's origins have been an open debate between scholars, with some believing that she was a demigod or a Jotunn rather than an actual deity. Most agree, however, that she is the daughter of the god Loki (the trickster) and the giantess Angrboda. She had two siblings, Fenrir, the wolf, and Jormungandr, the world serpent, both also the offspring of Loki.

Hel's outer appearance was unique. Scholars describe her as half-blue, like a giant, and half-flesh-colored, like a normal human. The duality of her appearance was thought to represent her two roles: as a patron of death and a guardian of the souls. In other tales, she is shown as a great beauty, with long flowing hair and a ghostly complexion. She was thought to be brutal, harsh, and menacing.

## The Underworld

The name itself, "Hel," means *hidden* or *to cover* and is a term to describe the afterlife and the souls of the dead since they cannot be seen by the living. The kingdom was often referred to as "Niflheim," which roughly translates to the world of darkness.

Norse mythology places the dwelling of the dead right below one of the roots of the world tree, "Yggdrasill." In some stories, it is thought that Niflheim was the last of the nine realms where all the wrongdoers ended up. Others believed a guard dog named Garmr presided over the entrance of Hel, not unlike the Greek tales of the three-headed hound Cerberus. The Norse dog would howl at the arrival of new souls.

The kingdom where she ruled was said to lie downwards and northwards. The logic behind that is that people are buried below the ground, and the cold in the north resembles the frigid nature of the land of the dead. Niflheim or Hel was divided into separate sections, one of which was the shore of corpses," Nastrond." In Nastrond stood a huge castle swimming in serpent venom, where sinners such as murderers and adulterers suffered torment like none other. They were forced to endure the pain of having their blood sucked by the dragon Nidhogg when he wasn't snacking on the roots of Yggdrasil.

Other tales suggest that the land of Hel was not one of torment but rather a welcome reprieve for the frail and old, those who suffered the straw of death. Not all who died were sent to Niflheim. The drowned were claimed by the goddess Ran (the personification of the sea), the warriors were granted passage to Valhalla by Odin, and the common folk were taken to Folkvangr (field of the people), a land commanded by Freyja.

## Mythology

When Loki's children arrived, a prophecy was declared to the Asgardian gods that the three younglings would cause distress and peril to the remaining deities. In an effort to counter the prediction, the All-Father Odin, king of the Gods, made his way to Jotunheim to bring the children back to Asgard, where he could keep a close eye on them.

To an outside eye, these actions resemble a paranoid yet concerned grandfather looking to change the fate of his grandchildren. That was far from the truth. While it is a fact that Odin was paranoid, his actions were not that of a loving grandparent. Immediately after collecting them, the king tossed the young serpent Jormungandr into the sea. He then threw Hela into the dark realm of Niflheim, tricking her into thinking that by doing so, she would be granted power over the nine realms of Norse cosmology. In truth, she was only allowed control over the dead souls that were passed down to her in the void that is Hel. For reasons unknown, Fenrir was kept with Odin in Asgard. Years passed, and the young wolf grew so strong and huge that the other gods feared they would be no match for the canine if he decided to turn against them. They came up with a plan to trick him into wearing manacles made by the dwarves, which were then used to hold him down on an island where he was stranded and left alone. At the same time, the little serpent was no longer little. He, too, had grown so large that he encircled the realm of Midgard (Earth), where the mortals lived, earning him the name the world serpent. In the meantime, Hela was reigning as queen of the underworld, no closer to escaping her fate than her subjects were.

## Hel's Powers

Hels' abilities represent a paradox. Many view her as an evil spirit since she is a patron of death. However, in Norse mythology, she was considered a neutral, positive figure for taking on the role of caring for the souls of the deceased. Her powers were quite specific to the realm she commanded.

- **Ruled Over the Underworld**

Hela was in charge of allowing the souls into the land of the dead. She may have also been responsible for their judgment and the consequences assigned to them based on their deeds during their lives.

- **Shapeshifter**

Like her father, the goddess could change her appearance. Whether it is an eagle, a fox, or even a flurry of snow, she can probably take its form.

- **Command Over Life and Death**

The queen of the underworld had the ability to grant and take life, as she was the gatekeeper of the land of the dead. This power ensured that a balance was kept between the living and the dead.

## Hel's Symbols

Every deity from ancient mythologies is linked to a series of symbols based on their traits and duties.

- **A Spindle**

This item is represented in different cultures as a metaphor for spinning the thread of life and death. It is associated with Hel based on the fact that she was granted the ability to take life or give it back, as well as keep the balance between the realms.

- **A Sickle**

The sickle symbolizes the end or the cutting off of the thread of life, which again is closely linked to Hel's powers over the dead.

- **A Hound**

Dogs represent loyalty, protection, and the ability to guard dwellings. All of these are qualities that Hel was thought to possess.

- **A Dragon or a Serpent**

Apart from being the sibling of the world serpent, when snakes shed their skin, it symbolizes rebirth, which could also mean rebirth in another realm.

# Skadi

Skadi was a giantess.[38]

Skadi is not considered a traditional goddess. Like Loki, she was a giantess who hailed from Jotunheim. In Norse mythology, most giants were described as unpleasant to behold, rough, and downright ugly. However, Skadi seemed to break that stereotype. Despite her blue complexion and huge physique, she was said to have had the features of a goddess. This fact was perpetuated by the truth that the gods appreciated beauty and would not have welcomed her into their fold otherwise.

The giantess was connected with cold and the hunt. She was known as a master skier, often portrayed with her ski shoes, quiver, and arrows. Unlike the rest of the giants, she had a calm nature and was not quick to anger or pick a fight. The lack of these usual giant characteristics did not take away from her strength and fierceness.

While a lot of tales portrayed the giants as evil spirits out to wage war against the gods, Skadi was one of the few believed to be free of any malicious intent despite her harsh and obstinate nature.

Skadi was a fresh addition to Norse mythology, often dominated by male figures. An independent, unwavering, self-reliant female who knows what she's owed, she was never afraid to fight for it.

**Mythology**

Skadi was the daughter of the giant Thiazi, who was known for his enmity with the Gods of Asgard. Guilty of stealing Idunn's apples (in other stories, he was guilty of forcing Loki to kidnap the goddess of youth, Idun), the giant was hunted down by the trickster Loki, who then fooled him into turning into an eagle and then killed him (in other tales, it is said that Thor was the one who took his life). Another version of the story suggests that as Loki was rescuing Idun at the behest of the gods, Thiazi transformed into an eagle and gave chase to the god of mischief. As they closed in on Asgard, the remaining gods created a firewall in the sky and killed the giant.

Though fully aware of her father's misdeed, Skadi was furious at the consequences that befell him at the hands of the Gods. After donning her armor, she made her way to Asgard to confront them and demand compensation for killing her father. In an effort to abstain from conflict, the gods of Azgard offered the young giantess a marriage proposal. Intrigued, Skadi agreed to the deal on the condition that they make an effort to make her laugh. The gods tried many jokes, but they all fell flat. In the end, Loki tied one end of a rope to a goat and the other end to his private parts. Loki would squeal in pain whenever the goat moved, making

Skadi laugh.

When it came to the marriage arrangement, despite her beauty, none of the gods were enthusiastic about marrying a giantess from Jotunheim. To settle the matter, she was allowed to choose her suitor from the lineup of gods only by looking at their feet. Secretly, the giantess was infatuated with Balder, the most handsome and kindest of all the gods. While examining the god's feet, she made an assumption that the most beautiful pair would for sure belong to Balder. She was sorely mistaken. When the veil was removed, she found herself face to face with the god Njord, patron of the sea and wind. Njord was much older than Balder and already had two other children, yet he had no wife.

Grudgingly, the pair honored the deal and sealed the marriage on the same day. The newlyweds were at a loss as to where to live. Njord loved the sea and shores, and Skadi enjoyed her time in the mountains and snow. Initially, they agreed to stay in each location for nine nights at a time, but that wasn't good enough for either of them, and they were both miserable with the arrangement. Eventually, they agreed to part ways amicably, forgoing their happily ever after. There is a mix of opinions regarding the fate of Skadi's love life following her failed marriage. Some say she lived alone in her icy castle, skiing to her heart's content on the slopes of the mountains. Others say that she married Ullr, the god of hunting and skiing, with whom she shared a lot of common interests. In several tales, it is believed that she even took Odin as a mate and had she bore several sons with him.

What most tales agree upon is that the giantess maintained her position as a goddess despite not being born as one. Despite her father's bad blood with the Asgardians and her short-lived marriage, she remained on good terms with the gods, even ready to lend a hand when they needed it.

It is said that she played a part in torturing the trickster for the role he played in killing Balder. She took part in tying him to a rock with a snake presiding over him and dripping venom on his face.

Skadi is known to have sided with the gods during Ragnarok against the other giants led by Loki. She was one of the survivors who got to see the dawn of the new world following the end of the gods.

### Symbols

Skadi's name carries a lot of symbolism in and of itself. It is said that it is derived from the old Norse word "Skadi," meaning harm, which is a direct link to her being a giant, a race mostly associated with death, violence, and darkness, not to mention the start of her myth is all about avenging her father's death.

Another interpretation of the name suggests it comes from the Old High Germanic word "Scato," meaning shadow.

There is also an ongoing debate that her name is linked to Scandinavia, with some believing that she inspires the name of the land and others thinking that it's the other way around.

The goddess is also heavily associated with the mountains, snow, and hunting, not to mention her prowess in skiing. So naturally, her snow boots, bow, and arrow were symbols heavily influenced by her character.

It didn't matter whether people believed her to be a goddess or a giantess. Prayers and tributes were made in her favor so people wouldn't suffer harsh and unforgiving winters, specifically in the Norwegian mountains.

# Angrboda

Angrboda was Loki's first wife.[29]

Angrboda was yet another giantess from Jotunn and the first wife of the trickster Loki. She lived in a place called Ironwood (Jarnvid), which is a forest where the female Jotnar lived in Jotunheimr. Known as the mother of the monsters for giving birth to Loki's offspring Fenrir the wolf, Jormungandr the world serpent, and Hel, the guardian of the underworld.

Her name translates to "the one who brings grief," "she who offers sorrow," or "distress bringer." Names that foreshadow her dark influence in Norse mythology.

The goddess was often associated with chaos and destruction. Even though she is not mentioned as extensively as her counterparts in the Norse pantheon, that does not take away from the complexity and impact she had throughout the tales.

To be able to bear children such as Hel, Jormungandr, and Fenrir, you'd have to be a formidable character to start with. Her knowledge of magic and ability to recite prophecies was described in detail in the myths. Those gifts were often associated with the path of fate and destiny. It was also said that she could decipher the runes and see beyond the present into the future. Like many other deities, one of her notable talents included shapeshifting into various forms.

**Mythology**

The relationship between Angroboda and Loki was often a pain point when it came to her relationship with the rest of the gods. Even though they both loved each other deeply, and Loki had fathered all three of her children, in the eyes of the Asgardians, she was still a giantess. Loki's allegiance to the gods was always scrutinized due to his close relationship with his wife.

Considering her a threat, Odin ordered his son Thor to kidnap the giantess and bring her back to Asgard. The god of thunder complied and succeeded in capturing the mother of monsters. On her arrival, she was able to strike a deal with the gods: her freedom in exchange for giving up her children to the will of the gods. The Asgardians agreed to the exchange because they feared that her children were dangerous enough to bring upon them the end of the world, or the event known as Ragnarok.

Odin wasted no time in trapping Fenrir on an island, throwing Jormungandr in the sea, and imprisoning Hel in the underworld to rule over the dead. The gods were right to be nervous; Loki's children, especially Fenrir, played a huge part in bringing down the kingdom of Asgard. After breaking away from his chains on the Island, Fenrir howled at the doors of the underworld, releasing Hel's army of the undead. Fenrir is known to have fought a mighty battle with Odin prior to swallowing the all-father whole.

It is said that Angroboda participated in the battle against the gods in Ragnarok. Though her fate is uncertain, it is believed that she may have died during the march on the gods. Most scholars determined that she didn't get the chance to see the dawn of the new world that followed this cataclysmic event.

**Symbols**

Because her presence in Norse mythology and the stories that have been passed down through the generations is insufficient, her symbols are not common knowledge.

Angroboda was portrayed with hair the color of deep red blood, bluish skin, and a formidably muscular physique that resembled most giants of Jotunheim. She was an incarnation of misery and chaos, which is a common factor among the ice giants.

# Chapter 10: Embracing the Dark Goddess Within

By guiding you as you form a connection with the divine feminine, this chapter takes you through the transformative journey of embracing the Dark Goddess within. It will give you plenty of practice, tips, and advice on how to acknowledge the shadow self and connect with the dark feminine energy within you.

Embracing the Dark Goddess within.[80]

# Your Inner Dark Goddess

The inner Dark Goddess can be viewed as part of your psyche and spirituality, making it a crucial tool for spiritual explorations. While most people think of darkness as something inherently flawed and destructive, embracing your inner divine feminine can teach you that this isn't the case. In fact, much of your personality and successes in all areas of life come from a balance between positive and negative forces within you. Still, many suppress their dark side due to societal expectations and widely accepted beliefs and traditions. You may be surprised that you're drawn to the divine feminine, but you aren't alone. Many people have experienced this over the centuries because they were drawn to it by their inner darkness – and for a good reason. The Dark Goddess within you can serve as an inspiration for your spiritual practices and a wonderful source of empowerment in times of need.

Do you wonder how you will know the goddess is awakening within you? Here are the telltale signs of the inner goddess at work:

- You experience self-doubt and insecurity, which results in envy and jealousy
- You have an immense fear of rejection and failure
- You are overly sensitive and prone to excessive emotional displays
- You strive for perfectionism and are driven by an intense need for control
- You overreact when someone disrespects your boundaries
- You tend to dwell on the past
- You find it easy to get people on your side or make them do whatever you want

While some of these may sound like negative traits, by going on this journey of self-discovery, you can learn why your goddess manifests the way she does and how to turn her manifestations in your favor. Self-discovery is having a better understanding of your desires, needs, feelings, and personality. Embracing the goddess through this process helps you improve your well-being and make better decisions, gives you a sense of purpose, enables you to build resilience and healthier relationships, gives you a chance to identify all your strengths and weaknesses, discover your passions and values, and much more.

# Acknowledging the Shadow Self

You can work with your inner Dark Goddess in several ways. The psychological and spiritual approaches to working with and accepting the shadow self as a part of oneself vary and often depend on what goddess you identify with and what feels right for you in the present moment. Remember, the goddess, too, took different routes to embracing and showcasing dark and shadowy aspects.

Meditation and other mindfulness exercises, for example, are great ways to focus your attention on exploring the negative aspects of yourself (the manifestations of your shadow/inner Dark Goddess). On the other hand, positive affirmations can help acknowledge and accept the shadow traits, which may not be attractive but are all the more useful. All these practices can also serve as preparatory steps for forming a deeper connection with the inner goddess. They teach you how to tap into your intuition, which is central to spiritual communication (whether with your own inner spiritual self or a goddess).

Another recommendation is a practice called shadow work or shadow integration. Through this practice, you unpack the parts of your personality, thought patterns, complex emotions, and behavior you've been hiding. Unveiling the shadow hidden within the dark corners of your mind takes time, practice, and dedication. Through shadow integration, you explore why these parts of yourself are suppressed and how to find healthy ways to express them. Moreover, you'll transform these aspects of yourself into a controlled, disciplined expression of your darkness. Transferring the manifestation of your shadow from the unconscious to the conscious (so that it can assist you in navigating the world) is essential for embracing the Dark Goddess within and working with other dark feminine energies.

### Shadow Visualization Technique

This visualization technique will introduce you to shadow integration and lay a foundation for further work with your shadow self.

### Instructions:

1. Find a quiet place where you won't be disturbed - the exercise requires undivided attention.
2. Sit or lie down in a comfortable position and close your eyes.
3. Inhale through your mouth and exhale through your nostrils to relax.

4. As your mind struggles to settle, it will still wander for a few minutes (especially if you aren't used to deep relaxation/mindfulness exercises).
5. For the time being, allow your thoughts to run free without judgment.
6. Relax every part of your body. If you find it difficult to relax naturally, you can play some meditation music or sounds or burn incense in the background.
7. Once you relax, imagine yourself at a dark cave's entrance. Proceed to enter the cave.
8. As you walk through the entryway, you feel chilled air enveloping you.
9. You see a tiny light flickering in the distance and walk toward it. When you reach it, you see the light coming from a candle illuminating a shadowy figure standing behind it.
10. You instantly feel negativity coming out of the figure, yet you also feel drawn to it. Take note of where this ambiguity is mostly present in your body.
11. When you're ready, step closer to the shadow and ask them questions. Ask them who they are, if there is anything they want to tell or show you, or anything else you feel like asking.
12. You'll feel their answer deep within and realize the shadow is you. Take a mental note of who they say they are and what message they want to give you. This may be a negative feeling, memory, or thought you've been trying to repress for years.
13. Once you feel they've told you everything you needed to know or can handle at that time (it's okay if you can't handle embracing everything at once), let their image slowly fade away.
14. You can repeat this exercise many times. Each time you do, new insights will be revealed.

## Connecting and Awakening Your Inner Dark Goddess

Here are even more recommended practices, rituals, and exercises to connect and awaken your inner Dark Goddess and explore their shadow self.

### Working with Nature

The influence of the Dark Goddess can be felt everywhere in nature. Even walking barefoot in a small patch of grass will help you feel her magic. Take every chance you get to spend time in nature, even if it's for 10 minutes a day. If you live near a large body of water, and the weather allows it, go soak your feet and call on the goddess. Surround yourself with plants in your apartment if that's your only way of physically connecting with nature. Every bit helps you bond with the dark feminine.

### Journaling

Whether you use it as a standalone practice or combined with another technique, journaling can be a powerful shadow exploration technique. You can jot down your experience with integration exercises. You can also use it to document your progress as you bond with your inner Dark Goddess. Write every day and read what you wrote at the end of the week. It'll allow you to recognize thoughts and emotions you weren't aware of. Even if you aren't sure of what to write or feel like you don't have anything to write, take out your journal and give your inner darkness free rein to express itself without censoring. You may notice you suddenly have a lot to write about!

### Practicing Self-Cove

One of the best ways to embrace your shadow self is to practice self-love. By showing yourself some love, you're indicating that you're willing to embrace every part of yourself. Accepting yourself as you mean you're letting go of past burdens, making peace with your past mistakes and weaknesses, and giving your body, mind, and soul what they need the most.

### Dark Moon Meditation

The following dark moon meditation will take you on a journey toward meeting your inner Dark Goddess and awakening her energy.

### Instructions:

1. Find a quiet place where you can get comfortable and won't be disturbed. Settle your body and mind and take a few deep breaths.
2. Prepare your mind for a fictional journey into a forest - it can be a place you know but doesn't have to be. Following your instinct, find a clearing in the forest and light a fire.
3. After settling in front of the fire, set an intention to access the deepest parts of your soul. Take a deep breath and feel the air

travel in your body - first upward to your crown, then down to your feet, and into the ground.

4. Now you've awakened both the dark energy within you and the Earth. Feel it travel up to your heart and outwards, enveloping you.
5. Feel the energy field extend around you toward the perimeter of the clearing, keeping you safe from everyone and everything around you.
6. Now, think about your plans for the following months. Feel the energy these goals evoke in you and channel them toward the fire before you. Think about what these plans mean to you, how they'll change your life, and who they'll make you become.
7. Let yourself drift into a deeper state of consciousness. Suddenly, you find yourself in the dark, enveloped only by the subtle light of the dark moon.
8. Allow yourself to adjust to the darkness. As you do, you feel more awakened, and your heart and mind open to new experiences.
9. Let go of all your fears, doubts, and thoughts you've created as a result of past trauma. Feel yourself being open to the unknown. Enjoy the freedom it brings you. You're now connected with the dark feminine.
10. Let the dark energy connect with your heart and soul, empowering you to speak your truth. Feel the goddess rise upward to your heart and even further into the universe.
11. When you're ready, take a deep breath and let the images and sensation go. Feel reassured in the knowledge that you're now unafraid of the unknown.

# Chapter 11: Honoring the Dark Goddesses: Rituals and Practices

This final chapter offers practical guidance for those interested in actively engaging with the dark feminine deities. Ritual practices and patchwork can deepen your spiritual connection with the energy or the archetype of the Dark Goddesses. Besides teaching you how to do them, this chapter will also explain how to prepare for these practices.

## Preparation and Setting

Having a sacred place as a center for your spiritual practice has numerous benefits for your connection with the Dark Goddess energy or archetype. By building an altar or similar area of worship, you're creating a space for invoking the goddess. Having a consistent space for your practices will also help you focus on your intention (a basic step you will need to take to manifest any desire, including your need to connect with the Dark Goddess). While creating a sacred space for practice, you'll also learn the goddess's correspondences - all the while expressing your creativity. By bringing together the right combination of elements, you can create a space for yourself, embracing all of your spirit, which will undoubtedly appeal to the Dark Goddess. You'll also get the chance to connect with nature.

Building an altar creates a space for invoking your inner goddess.[81]

From where you position it to the items you place on it, there are a lot of details that go into creating a sacred space. First and foremost, choose a fitting place, ideally in a quiet area in your home. If you don't have much space, you can always set up a small corner on your dresser, vanity table, inside your closet, or on the windowsill. You'll also need to keep in mind your physical and mental safety and well-being. Working with Dark Goddesses might involve lighting a candle or fire. Never leave these unattended. You should also prepare yourself for the emergence of negative thoughts and feelings. Make sure you're ready for this. If you're struggling with mental health issues or notice them while practicing, stop and only continue after consulting with a mental health professional.

## Rituals for Connection

### Meditating with a Symbol

One of the easiest ways to connect with a Dark Goddess is through one of her symbols. Meditating with her symbols will help you get into the right mind space to manifest your intention of connecting with the goddess. Draw a symbol of the goddess you want to summon on a piece of paper, meditate, and draw in her energy.

**Instructions:**

1. Start by assuming a comfortable position in a quiet room at night. Make sure you won't be disturbed for at least 10-15 minutes.
2. Take the symbol in your hands and greet the goddess:
   *"Great Goddess, I greet you now*
   *The ruler of darkness and things unseen*
   *Caretaker of dark energies*
   *The divine feminine.*
   *I am ready to unite with you*
   *Please hear my summons and come to my side."*
3. Visualize the symbol in front of your eyes.
4. Take a few breaths and focus on feeling the rich energy source stemming from the symbol.
5. Feel the goddess's power reaching you, enveloping your body. Feel it hyping you up to face your upcoming challenges.
6. Continue focusing on the symbol's energy until you feel prepared to complete your meditation.
7. When ready, let the image fade away.
8. Exhale deeply, and let your mind return to your everyday thoughts.

## Journeying and Pathwork

Journeying and pathwork are both useful means to connect with Dark Goddesses on a deeper level. As they take you on a journey exploring thoughts and emotions, they foster self-reflection, especially if coupled with journaling.

The following meditation will help you meet and communicate with a Dark Goddess of your choice. You'll stay in one place for 8-10 minutes, so make sure to find a comfortable position and support for your back if needed.

**Instructions:**

1. Sit cross-legged on a mat. Rest your hand on your legs and make sure your back is relaxed without slouching.
2. Using your abdominal muscles, take three deep breaths. That way, your breathing becomes even deeper. Do it slowly with a long, audible sigh every time you exhale.

3. After the third exhale, examine your body to see if you're relaxed and comfortable or if you need to make any adjustments to your position.
4. Close your eyes and picture yourself walking along a dark, graveled path on a quiet night. Visualize a waning or new moon rising over the tree lines (the darker, the better).
5. Keep walking confidently forward in your vision, and try to revere in the solitude and companionship of the darkness around you. It's cold, and you can see the little puffs your breath makes in the chill of the late evening air.
6. As you walk, picture a flickering light up ahead of you. As you get closer, you'll see the light coming from far away. Walk toward it.
7. Next, visualize a small offering you're carrying in your hands. This could be anything you want to offer the goddess you're summoning.
8. Suddenly, the wind picks up, and you've reached your destination. A torchlit area surrounded by the vast darkness.
9. Take a deep breath and leave your offering while saying a quiet prayer to the goddess. As you do it, start focusing on your surroundings.
10. You suddenly pick up a source of energy in the air. If you feel unstable, visualize yourself grabbing something sturdy to keep yourself upright.
11. Now, picture the noise and the winds fading away and the night becoming silent and peaceful again. Your offering is now on the ground. However, as you turn slowly, you realize you're not alone.
12. You see the woman draped in a black cape approaching silently. After greeting her, feel free to look up at her face. See her eyes radiate with timeless wisdom.
13. Visualize her greeting and thanking you for visiting her in her sacred place. While she may look intimidating, you know you shouldn't be afraid of her because she is here to guide you through any difficulties you may face in the next stage of your life.
14. See the goddess turning away and slowly walking away from you. Take a deep breath, and let the journey take you back home. Take three slow, audible breaths to bring yourself back.

# Sample Rituals and Meditations

## Hekate Meditation at a Threshold

As a guardian of the crossroads, Hekate is the easiest to reach. Make sure the threshold you're using is undisturbed so you can focus on the exercise without interruption. Here is how to meditate with Hekate at a threshold:

1. Start at dusk, as it is another time of transition when the goddess's power to reach this world is at its strongest. Turn off all the lights and electronic devices nearby, and sit near the chosen threshold.
2. Lean your back against something supporting it, and place a cushion behind it. Take a deep breath and close your eyes.
3. Picture yourself walking uphill toward a small cottage. Stroll towards it, and don't fear entering it. Take a few deep breaths if you need to calm yourself.
4. See yourself entering a brightly lit cottage. As your eyes adjust to the lights, you'll see that the house is more spacious than it seemed from the outside. Suddenly, a female figure emerges and reaches what's revealed to be the crossroads.
5. See yourself smiling at Hekate as she smiles back at you and welcomes you with her nurturing energy. You can ask the goddess if there is anything she wants you to know as you start your journey together. If you aren't prepared to ask her anything, simply let her presence relax and empower you.
6. Let the image of Hekate disappear, but you can remain at the crossroads as long as you want to. You can even let yourself drift off to sleep if you wish.
7. When you're ready, leave the cottage. As you step outside, let yourself return to reality as you slowly open your eyes.

## Night-Time Meditation with Nyx

This night-time meditation focuses on embracing the dark energy of Nyx, which is why it should be performed deep into the night. For practical purposes, it is recommended to choose a place near your altar where you can place a candle and light it for Nyx.

### Instructions:

1. After lighting a candle for the goddess, turn off all the lights and sit in a comfortable position.

2. As you exhale, let go of any tension from your body and allow your mind to sink into a state of relaxedness and serenity.
3. Take another grounding breath and prepare to travel into the deep night.
4. You suddenly see yourself in a lush, green, earthy meadow at night. You start exploring the field as the sounds of the night accompany you.
5. Visualize an entrance in a tree near the meadow. As you cross the entryway, you start feeling the divine energy reaching out to you, making you more confident in your purpose.
6. Picture the goddess standing before you, dressed in a black robe. She offers her protection, and you accept it. Take in her picture and know that just as she survived many challenges, so will you until your soul's journey in this life is over.
7. Before you leave her side, offer the goddess a small token of gratitude as an offering. This could be a thought of worthlessness, prejudice, or any negative emotion you want to leave behind.
8. To fill the space left behind by the negative thoughts and emotions, the goddess offers you her blessings. Take three deep breaths as you accept and embrace them.
9. Let the emotions her energy evokes come to the surface. Whatever you feel - sadness, rage, anxiety, etc. - embrace them in the here and now.
10. After thanking her, walk back through the meadow, slowly bringing your awareness back to the present.
11. Once you're ready, open your eyes and feel revitalized and filled with positive energy.

## Kali Invocation

The following Kali invocation will help you harness the goddess's energy when you feel the need for some internal purification. You'll need a representation of Kali.

### Instructions:

1. Find a quiet space, light a candle for the goddess, and relax by breathing deeply for 5-10 minutes.
2. When you're ready, take three breaths to ground and center yourself. Then, visualize a bright light enveloping you.

3. Close your eyes and tell yourself you're safe and protected by the goddess.
4. Think about what upsets you, bringing every thought, emotion, and belief into your consciousness. Do this for five minutes or as long as it takes to become fully aware of everything that worries you.
5. Open your eyes and look at Kali's representation. Focusing on every detail of the image before you, tell yourself what you see. Do this for three minutes, and feel yourself saturated with Kali's essence.
6. Chant Kali's name for another three minutes, close your eyes, and focus on your intention of invoking the goddess.
7. As you feel her energy uniting with yours, take a few minutes to sit with her.
8. When you are ready, thank Kali for coming to your side and offering her empowered alignment.
9. Affirm you are safeguarded by her energy, and let your eyes open slowly.

# Tables of Correspondences

## Hecate

The goddess of witchcraft, night, necromancy, and the moon.

**Equivalents**
- The Roman goddess Trivia.
- The Irish Triple goddess the Morrigan.
- The Mesopotamian goddess Ereshkigal.
- The ancient Egyptian god Heka.

**Colors**

Main Colors:
- Black
- Red

White Other Colors:
- Blue
- Yellow

**Offerings**
- Round cakes
- Fish
- Honey
- Milk

- Mead and red wine
- Pomegranates
- Candles (preferably in the colors associated with her)
- Almonds
- Sage
- Yew
- Obsidian
- Quartz
- Seashells
- Feathers from owls, crows, or ravens
- Images, drawings, or sculptures of the moon

**Symbols**
- Keys
- Torches
- Hecate's Wheel

**Moon Phases**

The waxing crescent, full moon, and waning crescent symbolize her Triple Goddess archetype. The goddess is also celebrated on the dark moon.

**Sacred Animals**
- Dogs
- Crows
- Snakes
- Ravens
- Boars
- Horses

**Sacred Numbers**
- 3
- 7
- 13

# Persephone

The goddess of Spring and fertility, and the Queen of the Underworld.

**Equivalents**
- The ancient Egyptian goddess Isis.
- The Norse goddess Hel.

**Colors**

Main Colors:
- Green
- Gold
- Red

Black Other Colors:
- Yellow
- Indigo
- Purple

**Offerings**
- Pomegranates
- A wreath of flowers.
- Roses, lilies, poppies, or other spring or wildflowers.
- Parsley
- Wheat
- Cypress
- Grains
- Honey
- Floral incense
- Boiled or smashed lemon balm, peppermint, or spearmint.
- Images or depictions of rams or bats.

**Symbols**
- Pomegranates
- Torches
- Grain seeds

**Moon Phases**
First Quarter
**Sacred Animals**
- Bats
- Rams
- Monkeys
- Parrots

**Plants**
- Pomegranate seeds
- Narcissus
- Lavender
- Willow tree
- Ivy
- Lily
- Daisy
- Maidenhair fern

# Nyx

The primordial goddess of the night in ancient Greece.

**Equivalents**
- The Roman goddess Nox.
- The ancient Egyptian goddess Nephthys.

**Colors**
- Black
- Dark Green
- Indigo
- Violet

**Offerings**
- Red wine
- Dark feathers
- Black tea

- Coffee
- Roses, poppies, lilies, and any dark flowers.
- Incense
- Resin
- Molasses
- Dark berries
- Dark chocolate
- Celestial symbols

**Symbols**
- Black wings
- Dark clouds
- Egg
- Stars
- Black fog

**Moon Phases**
New moon

**Sacred Animals**
- Owls
- Dogs
- Bats

# Sekhmet

The ancient Egyptian warrior goddess and the goddess of medicine.

**Equivalents**
- The Roman goddess Bellona.
- The Greek goddess Enyo.
- The Hindu goddess Kali.

**Colors**
- Red
- Orange
- Yellow

**Offerings**
- Red wine
- Incense
- Cat or lion depictions.
- Milk
- Fire
- Red gemstones like carnelian, garnet, and ruby.
- Spicy food

**Symbols**
- Red linen
- Lioness
- Sun disk

**Herbs**
- Catnip
- Basil
- Bay
- Patchouli
- Bloodroot

# Nephthys

The ancient Egyptian protective goddess of the air.

**Equivalents**
- The Greek goddess Nyx.
- The Roman Goddess Nox.

**Colors**
- Black
- Red

**Offerings**
- Incense
- Black cloth
- Wine

- Water
- Bread
- Flowers

**Symbols**
- Vultures
- Sycamore trees

**Sacred Animals**
- Snakes
- Vultures
- crows

**Plants**
- Sycamore fig tree
- Papyrus
- Persea tree

# Hathor

The ancient Egyptian goddess of the sky, women, love, and fertility.

**Equivalents**
- The Greek goddess Aphrodite
- The Roman goddess Venus

**Colors**
- Green
- Blue
- Black

**Offerings**
- Bread
- Wine
- Cheese
- Gemstones like malachite and turquoise.
- Copper and gold items.
- White, pink, or red candles.

- Jewelry
- Fabrics in her sacred colors.
- Mirrors

**Symbols**
- Cow
- Sun disk
- Sistrum
- Tree of Life

**Herbs**
- Rose
- Chamomile
- Myrrh
- Cinnamon
- Cider
- Jasmine

# Nut

The ancient Egyptian goddess of the sky and the guardian of the vault of the heavens.

**Equivalents**
- The Greek god Uranus.

**Colors**
- Blue
- Black

**Offerings**
- Water
- Bread
- Fig
- Grapes
- Incense
- Candles

- Lanterns

**Symbols**
- Stars
- Water
- Pots
- Wind

**Sacred Animals**
- Bunnies
- Frogs
- Bees

**Plants**
- Lotus

# Lilith

Mesopotamian figure of women's independence and freedom is associated with dark elements.

**Equivalents**
- Lamia from Greek mythology.

**Colors**
- Red
- Black

**Offerings**
- Candles in red, black, silver, and purple.
- Images or representations of the black moon.
- Owl and snake figurines.
- Paintings of the night sky and galaxy.
- Apples
- Red wine
- Apples
- Pomegranates

**Symbols**
- The triple moon
- The venus sign
- Wild rose

**Moon Phases**
Black moon

**Sacred Animal**
- Snake

**Herbs**
- Patchouli
- Wormwood
- Mandrake root
- Vervain
- Mugwort

# Inanna

The Sumerian goddess of war, love, and fertility.

**Equivalents**
- The Greek goddess Aphrodite
- The Greek goddess Athena
- The Roman goddess Minerva
- The Roman goddess Venus
- The Canaanite goddess Astarte
- The Canaanite goddess Anate

**Colors**
- Green
- Black
- Red
- White
- Silver

**Offerings**
- Libations
- Grains
- Bread
- Dates
- Honey
- Incense
- Flowers like roses and lilies

**Symbols**
- Lion
- Eight-pointed star

**Sacred Animals**
- Lions
- Doves
- Bats
- Snakes
- Butterflies

**Plants**
- Lilies
- Reeds
- Myrtle
- Narcissus

# Ereshkigal

The Sumerian horned goddess of the underworld.

**Equivalents**
- The Greek goddess Hecate

**Colors**
- Black
- Violet
- Dark brown

Offerings
- Bread
- Wine
- Beer
- Incense
- Pomegranate or lime juice
- Silver platters
- Plums
- Wheat
- Garlic
- Nutmeg

Symbols
- The cursing eye symbol
- The seven gates of the underworld
- Owls

Moon Phases
The dark and waning moon

# Baba Yaga

Equivalents
- The Greek goddess Hecate
- The Celtic mythological figure Cailleach
- The Celtic goddess, The Morrigan

Colors
- Black
- Brown
- Dark Green

Offerings
- Bread
- Pancakes
- Crepe

- Butter
- Milk
- Cheese
- Vodka or wine

**Symbols**
- Mortar and pestle
- Oven
- Skull and bones

**Moon Phases**
The dark and waning moon

**Sacred Animals**
- Crow
- Raven

# Marzanna/Morena

The Slavic goddess of death, rebirth, pestilence, and Winter.

**Equivalents**
- The Greek goddess Hecate
- The Greek goddess Demeter
- The Roman goddess Morta
- The Roman goddess Ceres

**Colors**
- Red
- White
- Black
- Green

**Offerings**
- Sickle
- Red and yellow apples
- Red beads
- Images of snakes and geese

- Stalks of grain
- A floral wreath
- Keys
- Honey
- Mead
- Beer
- Crystals

**Symbols**
- Birds
- Snakes
- Straw dolls

**Sacred Animals**
- Birds
- Snakes
- Frogs

**Plants**
- Grains
- Apple Trees
- Dyer's madder

# Kali

The Hindu goddess of darkness, destruction, and death.

**Equivalents**
- The Egyptian goddess Sekhmet.
- The Celtic goddess, the Morrigan.

**Colors**
- Black
- Blue
- Red

**Offerings**
- Red millet
- Gemstones like red tourmaline, smoky quartz, and labradorite
- Red or white flowers
- Incense like jasmine and sandalwood
- Bananas
- Coconut

**Symbols**
- Sword
- Trident

**Moon Phases**
The dark and new moon

**Sacred Animals**
- Tiger
- Lion

**Plants**
- Hibiscus
- Narcissus

# Durga

The Hindu goddess of war, destruction, and motherhood.

**Equivalents**
- The Greek goddess Athena
- The ancient Egyptian goddess Sekhmet

**Colors**
- White
- Red
- Blue
- Yellow
- Grey
- Orange

- Green

**Offerings**
- Sugar
- Traditional dishes like halwa and puri
- Red hibiscus flowers
- Jaggery
- Milk
- Coconut

**Symbols**
- Trident
- Conch shell

**Moon Phases**

The waxing moon

**Sacred Animals**
- Tiger
- Lion

**Plants**
- Rice plant
- Banana
- Arum plant
- Pomegranate
- Colocasia
- Sesbania sesban
- Wood apple
- Turmeric
- Ashoka tree

# Chinnamasta

The Hindu goddess of divine feminine energy.

**Colors**
- Red
- Black

**Offerings**
- Flowers
- Incense
- Fruit
- Sweets

**Symbols**
- Sword

# Chamunda

She is believed to be an aspect of the goddess Durga and is associated with transformation, protection, and destruction.

**Equivalents**
- The Hindu goddess Durga

**Colors**
- Red
- Black

**Offerings**
- Red or black flowers
- Incense, particularly jasmine or sandalwood
- Fruit
- Sweets

**Symbols**
- Trident

**Elements**
- Fire

# Oya

The Santeria goddess of storms, lightning, and death.

**Equivalents**
- The Greek god Aeolus

**Colors**
- Brown
- Burgundy
- Purple

**Offerings**
- Plums
- Eggplant
- Red wine
- Meat
- Dark chocolate
- Crystals
- Cherries
- Grapes
- Plums
- Spicy food

**Symbols**
- Thunderbolt
- Niger River
- Wind
- Fire

**Sacred Animals**
- Vultures

**Plants**
- Croton plant

**Sacred Numbers**
- 9

# Yewa

The Santeria goddess of death and virginity.

**Colors**
- White
- Pink
- Scarlet

**Offerings**
- Fish dishes
- Flowers
- Burgundy or black candles
- White wine
- Sweets

**Symbols**
- Bodies of water
- Pink veils
- Gravestones
- Cowry shells
- Mirrors

**Moon Phases**

Full moon

**Sacred Animals**
- Owl
- Fish
- Dolphins

**Plants**
- White lotus
- Lilies
- Chrysanthemums
- Orchid

**Elements**
- Water

# Ala

The Igbo goddess of earth, morality, and fertility.

**Equivalents**
- The Roman goddess Ceres
- The Roman goddess Juno

**Colors**
- Red
- Brown

**Offerings**
- Kola nuts
- Yams
- Meat
- Palm wine
- Fruits

**Symbols**
- Yams

**Moon Phases**
- The crescent moon

**Sacred Animals**
- Python

**Elements**
- Earth

# The Morrigan

The Irish goddess of war, witchcraft, and death.

**Colors**
- Red
- White

- Black
- Purple
- Indigo

**Offerings**
- Meat
- Apple
- Wine
- Feathers

**Symbols**
- Crows
- Ravens
- Feathers
- Candles
- Swords
- Axes
- Spears
- Shields
- The Moon

**Moon Phases**

The dark moon

**Sacred Animals**
- Wolves
- Cows
- Horses
- Scavenger birds

**Plants and Herbs**
- Belladonna
- Vervain
- Ginger
- Red clover

- Mugwort
- Thyme
- Blackthorn

# Macha

The Celtic goddess of war.

**Colors**
- Red
- Green

**Offerings**
- Grain
- Milk
- Cheese
- Butter
- Apples
- Mead

**Symbols**
- Horses
- Crowns
- A sheaf of wheat

**Sacred Animals and Plants**
- Horses
- Grains
- Wheat

**Elements**
- Earth
- Water

# Badb

The Celtic goddess of war and sovereignty.

**Colors**
- Black
- Red

**Offerings**
- Meat
- Fruits
- Wine

**Symbols**
- Crows
- Ravens
- Spears
- Cauldrons

**Moon Phases**

The dark and waning moon

**Elements**
- Earth
- Air
- Water

# The Cailleach

The Celtic goddess of the cold and winds.

**Colors**
- Blue
- White
- Grey

**Offerings**
- Stones
- Whiskey

- Bread
- Oatcakes
- Items made of wool or fiber

**Symbols**
- Staffs
- Cauldrons
- Stones

**Moon Phases**
The dark and waning moon

**Sacred Animals**
- Hares
- Deer

**Elements**
- Earth

# Hel

The Norse goddess of death and the underworld.

**Colors**
- Black
- Grey
- Dark blue

**Offerings**
- Coins and items of value
- White lilies
- Food and drink

# Skadi

The giant wife of the god of the sea in Norse mythology.

**Colors**
- White
- Silver
- Blue

**Offerings**
- Meat
- Fish
- Stew
- Bread
- Crystals

**Symbols**
- Skis
- Snowflakes
- Hunting gear

**Sacred Animals and Plants**
- Wolves
- Evergreen trees

# Angrboda

The bringer of grief in Norse mythology.

**Colors**
- Brown
- Green

**Offerings**
- Meat
- Mead
- Incense
- Stews
- Stones

**Symbols**
- Wolves
- Serpents
- Dragons
- Mountains

**Elements**
- Earth

# Conclusion

The fascination with ancient cultures will never stop. History, mythology, religion, and culture have always intrigued the world. One of the most interesting parts of diverse cultures is their deities. Some people feel connected to either a god or a goddess. If the Dark Goddess is calling for you, your life will be transformed in more ways than one.

You started this book by learning about the concept and significance of the Dark Goddess and how it can be a powerful force of transformation. You also discovered its meaning, symbolism, and origins and how the archetypes and shadow self are associated with the Dark Goddess.

You then moved on to explore Dark Goddesses from every ancient culture. You started with the often misunderstood Greek goddesses Hecate, Persephone, and Nyx and their archetypal themes and characteristics.

Ancient Egypt is filled with mysteries. Learning about their deities will take you a step closer to uncovering their secrets. You discovered the mythology behind each Dark Goddess and their association with war, chaos, and death.

You then went on a journey to the world of two fascinating ancient cultures: the Mesopotamian and the Slavic. You explored the attributes, myths, and legends associated with them.

Ancient Hindu culture has been influential, but many people aren't familiar with their deities. You discovered the Dark Goddess's key characteristics, symbolism, and popular forms. You then traveled to ancient Africa and learned about their Orishas and the spiritual aspects behind them.

The Celtic and Norse cultures are very popular, and many people are familiar with their deities. However, less is known about their Dark Goddesses. You uncovered the mystery behind them as well as uncovering their mythology.

Finally, you learned about embracing the Dark Goddess within and connecting with the divine feminine. You discovered the psychological and spiritual approaches of the shadow self. You also learned rituals and practices to honor your Dark Goddess and deepen your connection with her energy.

# Part 2: Black Madonna

*Unlocking the Secret Spiritual Power of the Mother Goddess*

# Introduction

The Black Madonna is an enigmatic icon. With her warm heart, deep eyes, and dark skin, she draws the hearts of millions across the globe. This being, known for healing many illnesses and emotional pain, transforming many lives, and inspiring peace, is revered and honored by many as a loving Mother Goddess. She welcomes one and all into her fold, fights to protect the people who place their trust in her, and offers her unparalleled wisdom and guidance in all things, great and small.

If you're interested in spirituality, you'll enjoy reading this book. It is packed with ancient wisdom explained in a way that the modern mind can grasp. These pages are an introduction to the Black Madonna, the Dark Mother who nurtures and cares for all. If you are drawn to the symbolism she represents and seek something beyond the usual traditional religious boxes that bind you, the odds are you are about to find everything you've always wanted.

The writing in this book is easy to understand. Typically, esoteric and spiritual matters are written in a language that makes it tough to grasp fundamental concepts, let alone put them to good use in your life. You'll be pleased to find that this book is nothing like that. Whether you've always known about the Black Madonna and have a fine grasp on matters of spirit, or you're just getting your feet wet with the subject, you'll find lots of lovely gems within these pages. The wisdom offered to you is practical, so you know how to take what you learn and use it to transform your life.

Are you ready to receive the love, healing, protection, and guidance you've always sought? Are you prepared to experience true, living spirituality under the loving guidance and instruction of the Black Madonna? Are you eager to know her? Well, your journey begins with the first chapter.

# Chapter 1: Who Is the Black Madonna?

You have picked this book because you want to know the Black Madonna. Something deep inside you is stirring, responding to her call. You may feel uncertain about who the Black Madonna is and if she is of any relevance to you. However, by the time you have read this chapter, you will come to know her essence, and should you choose to let her, you will experience her presence in your life in a powerful way. Before shedding light on who she is, you must understand what the Divine Feminine is about.

## The Divine Feminine

What is the Divine Feminine about? Divinity expresses itself in masculine and feminine ways. These energies are present in everyone and everything in creation. If you think about it, you can see this duality played out in every facet of life. There's day, and then there's night. You have light, and you also have darkness. There are the concepts of hot and cold, high and low, big and small, order and chaos, and yin and yang.

The Divine Feminine and Divine Masculine supersede the basic concept of gender. Instead, they represent specific traits and archetypes that are very real and observable in your daily life. Regardless of your gender, you carry these two energies within you. What sets you apart from another person is the unique ratio of feminine to masculine energy you express, and even that varies depending on the context you're looking at.

The mental processes you're blessed with are powered by masculine energy, while the feeling processes are the domain of feminine energy. You could think of masculine energy as being direct, moving from the inside to the outside, providing security, and giving of itself. As for feminine energy, it's not a straight line but a circle. The divine feminine energy goes within. It is a force that nurtures one and all, and rather than give, it is receptive. So, where the Divine Masculine is about creating, doing, and acting, the Divine Feminine is about receiving, being, and allowing. This book is about the essence of the Divine Feminine. It doesn't suggest the Divine Masculine has no use. So, the focus will only be on the person who has drawn you to this book.

People who have experienced the power of the Divine Feminine in their lives have nothing to share but positive testimonies of this force in their lives. She is the energy that teaches you to trust, to rest securely in your faith that your desires are accomplished and will manifest exactly when they should and not a moment too soon or too late. She is power. She is love. She is the essence of what it means to be. Everything you do in life stems from the state of simply being. She is a reminder to embody the version of yourself you'd like to be so that you can experience yourself as this person, and life can affirm that this is who you've become.

When you recognize and honor the Divine Feminine, you'll find you live a life free from force. You know you don't have to do too much to attract whatever you desire because you're co-creating with universal forces. You develop an awareness of being one with everything; therefore, you know that you draw whatever your state of being resonates with automatically. The Divine Feminine is the power that drives intuition, helping you know what you need to in inexplicable, and some would say illogical ways. She teaches you to transcend the prison of logic and trust that your every need is sorted even before you realize you have that desire.

Within the Divine Feminine, there's no way you could be desperate. You don't have that needy, pick-me energy. You not only recognize abundance in your life but experience it on a moment-to-moment basis. When you are drowning in self-doubt, you aren't expressing the Divine Feminine. Those lower vibrations are the Wounded Feminine. However, all wounds can be healed. All you have to do is open yourself up to the feeling of ease. Allow yourself to flow with life, and life will flow through you. How can you allow this energy to bless you? By choosing to trust more, relax more, and receive more. Choose rest over stress.

The Divine Feminine rules life's cycles. Whether it's the different phases of the moon, the rotation of seasons, or the planting and harvesting of crops, she embodies these cycles. If you contemplate them, you'll find that they happen automatically, and these cycles are the embodiment of birth, growth, death, and rebirth. This force connects to the earth and all things of the natural world. She reminds you that you are not separate. There's a connection between everything about you and the world around you. When you understand this, you'll begin to take care of your environment, and that's a good thing.

## Meet the Black Madonna

The Black Madonna is the epitome of the Divine Feminine.[39]

Now, it's time to answer the question that's been burning in your mind. The Black Madonna is the epitome of the Divine Feminine. She is not fictional. She is a very real presence, so much so that many are drawn to pay honor to her. In Switzerland, there is the Black Madonna of Einsiedeln. Every year, at least 500,000 people beat a path to her door to pay their respects to her. In Spain, the Black Madonna of Montserrat draws at least a million souls who come to thank her for her kindness and grace upon them. Poland's Black Madonna of Częstochowa sees 4 million people each year. In case you wondered, yes, there are even more statues and depictions of this melanated Mary all over the world. She inspires awe. Her power is unmistakable. Once you get to know her, it is impossible for your life to remain the same. You will experience her extraordinary grace and goodness each day.

What is it about the Black Madonna's art that fascinates many and captures their hearts? Is it simply because she's shown to be the Mother of Christ, the savior? Also, how is it that Mary, the mother of God, who has been stereotypically depicted and generally accepted as white in the West, is seen by others as being black? The answer to this mystery can be traced back to the period between the 12th and 14th centuries. During this time, many would devote themselves to Marian cults, in which Mary and Christ were honored. The Catholic Church recognized this and decided to place her at the center of the faith, never mind that ever since 431, she hadn't been recognized as divine, thanks to the Council of Ephesus ruling against that. This woman, who wasn't regarded as important, would become the one people reached out to in prayer, hoping for her healing touch. They knew she could offer them guidance in all their affairs. With time, there would be Marian cults that had depictions of the mother of God with black skin all over Europe. There was a stark difference in her depiction other than the distinction in skin color. The black Mary didn't appear as demure and innocent as the white one. She seemed to be something far more, carrying much more powerful spiritual significance than her Catholic counterpart. It was undeniable to one and all that the Black Madonna was the true Madonna with unquestionable power.

There's some debate about why these depictions of Christ's mother were black. Some historians insist the only reason they're that way is because of layers of incense soot accumulated over the years. They believe the blackness is a result of candles singeing the images and statues gathering grime from being kept underground. Their point is the Black Madonna was never black at first but only gradually became so. However, that's not accurate. There's evidence to show the people of that period made a deliberate decision to paint her black, and even if she were discolored, they deliberately kept her that way.

It is laughable to suggest that the Black Madonna is a mistake. Marion Woodman and Elinor Dickson are two Jungian theorists who propose that there are two factors that led to the creation and adoption of this benevolent being. Western European Christians had taken it upon themselves to go to war against Muslims because they were concerned about the Muslims taking over the Middle Eastern Holy Land, and they wanted to take back the places that used to be Christian. These wars are known as the Crusades, and as a result of the plundering, Europe would come to discover images and figures of the Black Madonna. Inanna and Isis presented fresh ways to view the archetype of the goddess, and naturally, European artists began depicting the Madonna in the same style. The second factor Woodman and Dickson recognized is the effect of the combination of the adoption of courtly love and the Marian cult. What was that? People became fascinated by the concept of the "idealized woman." Before this time, the white Mary was the representation of that concept. The people needed something to match that, and so the Black Madonna couldn't have come at a better time.

The blackness of this deity makes her important. Many assume darkness has to do with the bad, the unknown, the things lurking in the shadows waiting for a chance to ruin you. However, black had a more generous meaning during the Middle Ages. The difference between black and white wasn't an oversimplification that boiled them down to good and bad. When you consider black from the feminine perspective, you realize it's about more than that. The Black Madonna is the embodiment of the flow of life, which includes death and rebirth. So, death isn't considered a bad thing but necessary for life to continue. The Middle Ages people craved something far deeper and more potent than that offered by the standard Virgin Mary. They wanted a connection with the Goddess, and they got it. The traditional depiction of the Virgin Mary didn't quite work. After all, the only reason she was recognized as a divine being by the Church was to be the token female for a group of men who didn't care much about women or nature. On the flip side, the Black Virgin represents nature and its power to heal one and all. She represents the power of the female, long ignored and downplayed. Where the Virgin Mary is all whiteness and purity, the figure of a doting mother caring for Jesus as a baby, the Black Madonna is the embodiment of the sensuality of womanhood. You can either find her alone or with Jesus in her arms and a face that gives the impression of gravity and dignity. The Black Madonna's fierce independence is the reason many hearts are drawn to her.

# The Meaning of Black

The Black Madonna is also called the Dark Mother, the African Mother, or the Black Virgin. She's always black. When she's carrying the baby Jesus, he's depicted as black, too. The Black Madonna has many historical and cultural influences, but her beginnings are African. You could say African traditional and spiritual beliefs have had a strong impact on the major religions practiced across the globe, namely Judaism, Christianity, Islam, and Hinduism. The Black Madonna is a connecting thread, weaving her way through each religion and spiritual tenet. There are various ways in which the black skin of the Black Madonna is significant.

**The Divine Feminine:** The black skin of the Dark Mother represents the Divine Feminine's essence. This energy contains all things mysterious and deep. It carries the mysteries of life that no mind has grasped yet and which is responsible for keeping one and all alive. It is a reminder of the darkness of the womb from which you and everyone else emerged. This darkness is where all life springs from. Even when planted, seeds are covered in the ground, left to grow in darkness before they spring up to the light. The black skin demonstrates the power of the Divine Feminine to nurture you, transform you into something more, and restore you when you're worn out.

**The Process of Creation and the Concept of Fertility:** Black is the color of fertility. It is the epitome of riches. Consider, once more, the seeds left in the darkness of the Earth only to bear more life. The Black Madonna's skin is a reminder of the eternal principles of growth and renewal. Allow it to demonstrate that you have the power to create whatever you desire in life, and as long as you trust in that, you will enjoy continuous transformation for the better.

**The Power of Embracing Your Shadow Self:** No one is all light and goodness. The principle of duality is active even when it comes to how you live your life. The Goddess's black skin encourages you to take a look at your shadow aspect. It tells you that while you may be tempted to run away from your doubts and fears, it is within them you will find healing, and only by facing them can you experience growth in life. So, the African Mother is inviting you to dive into the raging storms within yourself because you will be rewarded for your bravery and willingness to embrace your shadow self.

**The Definition of Inclusivity.** Where the white Virgin Mary only catered to one group, the Black Madonna is universal. She is no respecter of race or culture, as her grace extends to one and all. Her black skin is the true meaning of inclusivity and a reminder that the Divine Feminine is for one and all, not a select few. She breaks down all barriers and divisions, uniting all of humanity under one umbrella. Africa is the cradle of life, so the Dark Mother's skin is a reminder that she is the original mother of all children of the Earth.

## Many People, One Mother

The Dark Mother has undeniable global influence. Many are aware of her miracles and are happy to testify of them, spreading news of who she is and what she has to offer to the souls who put their trust in her. She has many pilgrims devoted to her for good reason. In Algeria, she is Our Lady of Africa. In Côte d'Ivoire, you can find the Black Madonna with Child in the Basilica of Our Lady of Peace in Yamoussoukro. Those from Senegal call her *Notre Dame de la Délivrance*, which means "Our Lady of Deliverance. In Soweto, South Africa, she is simply The Black Madonna.

What about the Philippines? There, she's known as *Nuestra Señora de la Paz y del Buen Viaje de Antipolo,* which means Our Lady of Peace and Good Voyage of Antipolo. They also call her *Nuestra Señora de Guía* (Our Lady of Guidance), *Nuestra Señora de los Desamparados* (Our Lady of the Abandoned), *Nuestra Señora del Buen Suceso* (Our Lady of the Good Event), *Nuestra Señora de Regla* (Our Lady of the Rule), *Nuestra Señora de la Peña de Francia* (Our Lady of Penafrancia), *Nuestra Señora de la Visitación de Piat* (Our Lady of the Visitation of Piat), or *Nuestra Señora de la Salvación* (Our Lady of Salvation). These are only some of the names she goes by in this region, and it's by no means an exhaustive list. You can find her all over the world, from Africa to Asia and Europe to North and South America. That should make it clear she is revered as a mother goddess.

The interesting thing about the Black Madonna's names is that they are containers of her essence. For instance, she is called Our Lady of Deliverance for a reason. On account of her extensive reach across various cultures, countries, and spiritual practices, the Black Madonna is the true embodiment of unity. She is someone who is open to one and all, the true universal figure. Her compassion is available to you regardless of who you may be. She doesn't play games. She's not interested in favoritism. You know that wherever you are in the world, you can access her love.

An interesting thing to note about most religions is how the idea of exclusivity is often present. In the sacred pages of religious texts, you find messages that indicate God has set apart a certain set of people from the rest of the world. It's natural to feel like you don't matter as much as these people if you are not one of them. However, the Black Madonna is the answer to this ostracism, which is unnecessary. The Black Madonna is only interested in the language of the soul, in which everyone is fluent. Whether you cry out to her or whisper what you desire, she's always there to listen and assist you.

Need to walk the path of the Black Madonna? You realize that all souls are equal in her eyes. It doesn't matter what your age, gender, or social status is. She doesn't care about your personal history. She couldn't care less about how much money you have in your bank account or if you're old and wrinkly or young and inexperienced. As long as each time you approach her, you keep an open heart and come from a place of sincerity, you can engage her in a sacred dialogue, and she will respond to you in the way you need.

## Keeper of Secrets of Spiritual Power and Transformation

The Black Madonna has secrets that have long eluded many, especially regarding spiritual power or the ability to transform your life into whatever you please. This goddess is strongly connected to ancient traditions where the Divine Feminine was honored. Thanks to these ancient connections, you can turn to her for spiritual knowledge on how to use the power of spirit to create the life of your dreams. This being is a teacher of the process of divine alchemy. Since she is the raw material (or *prima materia*), you need to exercise spiritual power and bring powerful change in life. No one would know better than she how to progress toward enlightenment.

The African Mother is the marriage of light and dark. She shows you how these forces are within you, regardless of whether you've acknowledged it. You can't always be one way or another, so she reminds you there's nothing wrong with that. You have two sides to yourself. If you take her wisdom to heart and embrace both seemingly contradicting sides of yourself, you'll be wiser and better for it.

Whether you seek healing, guidance, protection, or anything else, you can always turn to the Black Madonna, and she will help you. Historically, there have been many stories about her assisting people who are suffering, whether physically or otherwise. She is the embodiment of the process of transformation. You can do everything that you must in order to manifest the life that you desire. However, to ensure you experience as much ease and flow as possible, you should connect with the Black Madonna. If you're wondering if you have the right to connect with this deity, as mentioned before, she does not care about where you are from or who you identify as. As long as you approach her with a sincere heart and a desire to be touched by her grace, you will experience miracles.

# Chapter 2: Her Sacred Artistry

## The Universality of Art

The beautiful thing about art is that it is not limited by language. That's what makes it such a profound medium for taking abstract concepts and spiritual matters and translating them into things that many can look upon and understand in an instant. There is no better medium of expression than art. Whether it's a sculpture or a painting, everyone can understand the emotions and ideas that a particular work of art conveys. Expressing spiritual concepts using art is the process of taking the intangible and making it real so that you can relate to it on a level you understand. The moment you set your eyes upon a work of art, you create an emotional connection between yourself and that work. What you take away from what you see depends on you.

Art is a universal language heavily reliant upon emotion and imagination. Regardless of which language you speak or where you're from, you have the ability to imagine. You also feel emotions like everyone else. Since art is rooted in these two things, it makes it easy to connect with it on a personal level. That's why when you are looking at a work of art that depicts the Black Madonna, you will experience a deep connection to her.

Art is a mirror, showing how the world has been in the past and what it's like at present. Some people are quick to dismiss art as being unimportant. That would be a big mistake. Within a work of art is the spirit of the time and the place it was made. It represents what people believed and what they valued. So, when you're looking at a visual depiction of the Black Madonna, regardless of what culture or era it's from, you get a sense of how the spiritual lives of the people in those times evolved around this figure.

There is no better way to create the experience of a shared connection than through art. It isn't bound by geography. It isn't restricted by culture. So, everyone gets the chance to connect to the art in their personal way. When you look upon a Black Madonna's depiction or contemplate it, you find yourself connecting with the Divine Feminine. That work of art is a bridge of sorts. It helps connect the profound and the profane, the sacred and the regular.

## Artistic Representations of the Black Virgin

For centuries, there have been many depictions of the Black Virgin or Black Madonna worldwide, especially in Latin America and Europe. You'll notice that the images are statues like the Mother Mary with her child Jesus, except that they have dark skin and hair.

The Black Madonna of Montserrat represents hope for those who come before her.[33]

The Black Madonna of Montserrat is a statue from the 12th century. You can find it at the Benedictine monastery in Catalonia, Montserrat, Spain. This statue is a unique one carved from black wood, and it's one pilgrimage site that many loyal devotees of the Black Madonna love to visit. The Black Madonna of Montserrat represents hope for those who come before her. She promises comfort to those who suffer and need relief from their burdens.

In Częstochowa, within the Jasna Góra Monastery, you'll find the Black Madonna of Częstochowa, a depiction of the Black Virgin and the baby Jesus. The African Mother is painted on wood and then covered in a coating of gold and silver. There is no goddess or divine being more venerated in Poland than the Black Madonna of Częstochowa. For many of the people in Poland, she represents the Polish identity. She also represents the spirit of resistance. Many of the great revolutions that led to a better way of life came about as a result of people willing to resist the status quo. So, for the Polish, their artistic depiction of the Black Madonna embodies this energy.

How about the Black Madonna of Guadalupe? This image is from the 16th century and shows both Mary and Jesus. You can find this at the Basilica of Our Lady of Guadalupe, which is in Mexico City, Mexico. According to legend, this picture appeared miraculously on a cloak. It was a unique cloak made of cactus fiber.

Regardless of her characterization or its location, these representations typically carry a message about who the Black Virgin is. The fact that she is often portrayed as a black woman is a powerful thing to consider. She is the complete antithesis of everything traditional from a Eurocentric view. Since she is artistically depicted as black, this flies in the face of what is considered Christianity. It affirms the worth of everyone on the planet.

If you pay close attention to the artistic depictions of the African Mother, you'll notice she often demonstrates compassion. How? Observe the way she holds Jesus close to her bosom while she looks out at the people with gentle, kind eyes. Those who know the Black Madonna can trust her to serve as their protector and mother at all times. They are certain she is committed to interceding on their behalf. The Black Virgin is also artistically depicted in a way that demonstrates her humble nature and the power she carries. Her clothes are simple, and her expression communicates serenity and peace. Artists will often draw a halo around her, as well as other symbols that represent divinity to remind you that she is holy.

# Symbolism in Artistic Depictions of the Black Madonna

Artwork that depicts the Black Virgin uses symbolism to communicate the spiritual essence of this deity. Where the darkness of her skin represents her connection to humanity, the halo around her head represents her connection to divinity. When the Black Virgin is depicted as sitting on a throne with Jesus in her lap, it tells you she is the Mother of God and the Queen of Heaven. There are other depictions of the Black Madonna showing her holding on to the crucified body of Christ. When she is in this particular pose, it demonstrates her compassion for those who suffer.

Sometimes, the Black Virgin is depicted as wearing blue and white robes. The color blue represents grace. Some say it also symbolizes what it means to be pure, in the same way as white does. These colors demonstrate the essence of the Black Madonna.

She may also be seen with certain accessories, such as a crown. The crown is a reminder that she is the Queen of Heaven. When you see a depiction with a scepter in her hand, it reminds you she has authority over life. Did you know even her gestures are symbolic? When she has her hand raised, she's blessing you. When her hands are holding on to her child, Jesus, it represents the energy of nurturing and maternal love. Some depictions of the Black Virgin show her pointing toward you as if inviting you to connect with her energy so you can enjoy her protection and love. These are just a few elements of the different depictions of the Black Madonna in art.

# Connecting through Art

At this point, it should be obvious that the depictions of the Black Madonna are not ordinary. They are sacred and powerful tools that can act as portals to connect you to the spiritual world. Whether you decide to look at her art, create some art with her image, or meditate on her images, you can establish a connection to divinity and allow the Divine Feminine to flow freely in your life. You can tap into this by sitting with the art and observing it. The more you contemplate the art, the deeper meaning you will glean from it, which means you have a stronger connection to this deity. You can tell that you have a profound connection with the Black Madonna's art when you sense strong emotions within you.

If you want to express your devotion to the African Mother, you can also create art of her. As you create, you can meditate on what she means to you or what she's done for you. By choosing to create art, you express your spiritual side. The work you create is not ordinary either, as it becomes a portal for you to allow her energy to come through.

Are you uninterested in creating art? There are other ways you can honor and connect with the Black Madonna. For instance, you could meditate on her image. All you have to do is focus fully on her, and when you notice that your mind is wandering, return your attention to her image. As you do this, your thoughts quieten, and your mind feels peaceful. You can then focus on her energy and what she represents. Think about what you would like her to do in your life. Meditating on her image is enough if you are uncertain about what you would like the Black Madonna to do for you. As you do so, you will experience transformation. The Black Madonna knows what you need better than you. She is happy to assist you and bless you. As a bonus, many can testify to gaining spiritual insight when they meditate on her image. They receive guidance regarding specific situations or about their life in general. As a result, they experience transformation. You can experience the same thing.

## Stories and Legends

According to legend, the painting of Our Lady of Częstochowa was done by Saint Luke the Evangelist. It is said that this painting has the power to heal and has healed many. Pilgrims flock to the monastery by the hundreds of thousands annually because they hope the Black Madonna will touch them with her healing hands. In 1655, invaders from Sweden had set their sights on the Jasna Góra Monastery. Legend has it that the Black Madonna saved the monastery from these invaders.

In 937, Otto the Great created Magdeburg. He'd wanted the cathedral to have a Benedictine abbey in it. By 1207, The cathedral had to be rebuilt from scratch because it had suffered from a horrible fire incident. According to legend, only one statue remained standing with candles still burning before it, while everything else was reduced to ashes. What statue was that? The Black Madonna.

The Black Madonna of Guadalupe first revealed herself to a man called Juan Diego in 1531. She gave him very clear instructions to build a church on the Tepeyac hill. Juan made an astonishing discovery about the hill as he noticed that roses bloomed there when it was winter. So, he picked a few of those roses and put them in his cloak. Juan made his way over to the Bishop. When he handed the Bishop the roses, the man of the cloth would notice the face of the Virgin was on the fabric. The cloak still exists, kept safe in the Basilica of Guadalupe.

How about the Black Madonna of Einsiedeln? She is also called Our Lady of Hermits. Why is that? Because it was a hermit who discovered her back in the 9th century. His name was Meinrad. He was so enamored by her grace and goodness that he built her a chapel. Eventually, poor Meinrad would be murdered by robbers who wanted to keep the statue for themselves. What happened after this is a testament to the Black Madonna's justice. Two ravens tailed the murdering robbers. These birds then revealed to the authorities what these men had done to Meinrad, and justice was served. The statue would then be relocated to the monastery. There, people honor her for the protection she offers to travelers and pilgrims. These are just some of the stories and legends surrounding the Black Madonna. Even now, she continues to bless, guide, protect, heal, and nurture those who love her. People know the power they can use to better their lives through artwork representing the African Mother.

# Chapter 3: Her Themes and Symbolism

In this chapter, you are going to dive even deeper into the themes and symbolism connected to the sacred Black Madonna. There is so much more to this divine being. There are many rich and complex layers of significance found in her imagery. This chapter is written with the intent of helping you understand those meanings to use in your spiritual practice with her.

## The Divine Mother

When the Black Madonna is depicted as the Divine Mother, it resonates strongly with one and all because of the Archetype known as the Mother. Her motherliness shines through as she cradles her baby in her arms or holds on to the crucified body of the Savior, Jesus Christ. There is something deep in the human psyche that desires maternal love. When the chips are down, and things seem to not look great, some call out for their mothers or at least wish they could have her with them. There's a good reason for this.

Motherly energy is nurturing and feels like safety.⁵⁴

Motherly energy is nurturing and feels like safety. The Black Madonna is reminiscent of what it means to have motherly love and comfort. She is there to act as your shield. She is right there with you, and you are never alone, no matter what you're going through. A mother's love is unconditional. The same applies to the Black Madonna's love for you. She has a bond with her child that is unbreakable. You are her child. You are the representation of Jesus in her arms. She is dedicated to keeping you safe at all times.

Does it feel as though life has been terrible for you lately? Turn to the Black Madonna, and she will offer you the comfort you crave. Do you feel lost and need help knowing what the best option to choose in a situation is? You can depend on her motherly wisdom to guide you. Do you chronically feel unsafe no matter what you do? If you surrender to her, she will protect you day and night.

You can connect with her using her artwork. Understand that art is more than just art. It is the crystallization of her energy, which can and will act upon your life if you let it. Often, in depictions of her with her baby or with the crucified Christ, she has eyes full of love. She gazes at you softly, letting you know that she understands you. Her eyes invite you to come to her and find refuge in her arms. They tell you you don't have to go it alone. You can work with her guidance to feel more certainty and safety.

Her eyes carry the wisdom of a mother. What mother on earth could possibly top the Divine Mother?

## The Light and the Dark

Studying the artwork of the Black Madonna will reveal an interesting interplay of light and darkness. This is no accident. There are layers of meaning woven into the dance of light and darkness. For one thing, the Black Madonna has black skin. This is representative of the divine feminine and how it expresses itself. The blackness is the source of life, helping you to connect you to the power and mysteries of creation. All things that are created come from darkness first. Some people assume that darkness or blackness is a sign of ignorance or something that is not clear. These people couldn't be more wrong. The darkness in the artwork of the Black Madonna is a representation of spiritual insight and profound wisdom. Think of it like looking into a really deep well. At some point, you can no longer see what's at the bottom because of how deep it is. All your eyes can pick up on is blackness, but cleansing, refreshing water is within the well.

In the same way, the human mind can't comprehend fully or grasp the wisdom that the Black Madonna carries. Fortunately, you don't have to understand it fully. You only need to trust her ability to help you with whatever you need.

What about the light from the halo of the Black Madonna? Or the light that surrounds her? This isn't done only for artistic intentions but to represent a powerful spiritual message. When you are experiencing the dark night of the soul, you can count on the Black Virgin to bring you the light of revelation and insight. If you are used to feeling unsure and unclear about your life, you will receive clarity and inspiration by devoting yourself to her. The light aspect of the Black Madonna symbolizes the higher awareness you receive by choosing to walk a spiritual path with her as your guide. Life is complicated. It's not easy to figure out your place in the world or what you should be doing. However, by turning to the Black Madonna, she will guide you through the labyrinth of living. All you have to do is take her hand. Trust that she knows where you should go and it's a good place for you.

When you meditate on the interplay of light and darkness in the artistic depictions of the Black Madonna, you will find a powerful metaphor. Light and darkness represent the potential for you to grow and transform into something more beautiful than you are. These two elements demonstrate that you have the ability to come up through challenges and suffering and experience a better life. The cosmic dance between the two is a reminder of the poet Dinos Christianopoulos's saying, "They tried to bury us, but they didn't know we were seeds." Even if your life feels a little dark right now, by working with the Black Virgin, you will eventually break through the dark soil and into the light.

Another interesting thing about the interplay of light and darkness, as depicted in Black Virgin's artwork, is that there is power in suffering. No, this does not imply she would like you to suffer through life. She asks you to recall that each time you have gone through a challenge, you have been transformed into someone stronger and more resilient than you used to be. She wants you to remember that the trials you're going through are not the end of your story. Those struggles are a necessary part of your life's journey. Think of it like passing gold through fire to refine it so it can shine bright and brilliant. The light and darkness in the artwork of the Black Virgin is a reminder that you can grow, heal, and spiritually evolve when you embrace the lessons of your suffering.

## Suffering and Compassion

Her compassion knows no bounds.[85]

A deep analysis of the Black Madonna's artwork will also reveal prominent themes of suffering and compassion. This is especially the case when she is depicted as Mater Dolorosa, also called the Sorrowful Mother. There is a lesson here in how empathy, suffering, and compassion intertwine to create a narrative that inspires one and all. As the Mater Dolorosa, she represents the ancient archetype of the daily suffering humans battle. When life feels like a burden to bear, the Black Madonna is there with you, ready to be your help. She is full of empathy and understands the sorrows that you are experiencing. She desires nothing more than to be there, to wipe your tears away and lift the burden that weighs your back down and makes your shoulders droop. As the Mater Dolorosa, she has tears in her eyes, feeling the sadness, loss, and grief of all humanity.

The African Mother is bonded to you on an emotional level. She doesn't just see you when you're hurting. She feels every single thing you go through. Her compassion knows no bounds. Whenever you're feeling blue, you can look at illustrations of her as the Sorrowful Mother and draw strength and comfort from her. She wants you to know that you are not alone, and she will always be your companion when no one else is there for you.

The Sorrowful Mother loves you unconditionally like any mother would their child. She is willing, eager, and even desperate to reach out to you and take you into her loving arms. People who have experienced horrific events in life can testify to the depth of her love. The Black Virgin isn't some god high up in the sky, far away and removed from your pain. She doesn't just give you a trite statement like, "My ways are far more mysterious than you could ever understand," and expect you to be okay with that. She does everything in her power to make her comfort and solace as real to you as the words on this page.

The archetype of the Mater Dolorosa is a reminder that you can heal, but only when you choose to be compassionate. Most importantly, you must extend this compassion to yourself. Healing can only begin when you accept that you are in pain. It's not easy to admit your suffering. However, if you can face the truth and connect with the Black Virgin, you will find - in her - a space to grieve. You will find the space comforting. You'll realize she understands you more than anyone ever could. She is the one in the world who would never judge you and loves you unconditionally.

You don't have to be or do anything to receive her love. As you show compassion to yourself and allow the Black Virgin to demonstrate her compassion toward you, you will experience healing on every level. Your body will feel better. Your mind will perform better. On top of all that, if there are any emotions that you are struggling with, you will find relief from them. This is the definition of true, complete healing. This is what the Sorrowful Mother offers you.

## Healing and Transformation

Another popular way the Black Madonna is portrayed is as the Divine Mother, responsible for healing everyone. When she is present in your life, she may as well be a miracle balm, soothing and healing you in every way. If you want to experience her healing power, you can. Decide that you will surrender to her and trust that she will deliver a satisfying and fulfilling outcome.

The African Mother represents the idea of hope when things are not going well. You can draw strength from her if you feel tired and are unable to continue with whatever you're struggling with. Allow her to fill your heart with hope, and you will be amazed at how you can pick yourself back up and keep going. Her transformational power turns your tiredness into toughness. She takes your weaknesses and turns them into strengths. If you give her all your doubts and fears, she will transform those into certainty and trust. There is no transformer as powerful as the Divine Feminine, the Black Mother herself.

The Divine Mother is the original alchemist. She takes your human experience and upgrades it, helping you discover more of who you are. The more you discover yourself in her, the more resilient you become. When you are on a healing journey and decide to walk with the Black Madonna, you must first be at peace with the things you feel vulnerable about. What terrifies you? What has left you feeling lost and uncertain? Whatever those things are, you must be honest about them.

Why should you acknowledge these things? Accepting how you feel makes room for the Divine Feminine to work her alchemy on you. The truth about your insecurities, doubts, and worries is they are the fuel for the miracle you expect. They are the raw materials that the Divine Mother will craft into the results that you seek. You can allow this change to begin when you surrender to her. It starts from within and works its way outward, so everyone in your life will see that the Mother's touch has truly transformed you.

# Revealing the Goddess' Wisdom

Every brush stroke of a painting of the Black Madonna reflects the essence of the Divine Feminine. As you meditate on this art, you will peel back the layers to reveal various aspects of the Mother. The more you discover, the more you become the thing you discover. You are transformed into the image of the Mother, as wise, loving, nurturing, protective, and creative as she.

Look at all artwork depicting the Divine feminine as the Black Madonna through these lenses. As you do, you will discover the artwork is far more than simple artistic expression. You will learn that the figure of the Black Madonna is a deep well full of spiritual guidance and insight. You will experience and express her uncommon wisdom.

The more you allow yourself to dwell on the Black Madonna, the more you realize she is not your regular external deity. No one will be able to convince you otherwise. You will have experiences that show she is with you all the time. You carry her in the depths of your soul. You can't be separated from her. You may, at times, feel as if she is distant, but that is because you have closed your eyes to her presence in your life. As the Divine Mother, she can't abandon her own. You are one of hers, so whenever you feel alone or as if she isn't there, remember this.

By allowing yourself to soak up the insights you get from spending time in reflection and meditation on the Black Mother, you will discover your purpose. She is an endlessly flowing river of inspiration that you can draw from to your heart's content. Through her symbology, themes, and artwork, you'll discover that the Black Virgin is the one you have been searching for all your life.

# Chapter 4: Her Transformative Power

Before understanding the transformative power of the Black Virgin, it is essential to explain what it means to be transformed in spiritual and personal contexts. When you experience transformation, you notice that your life has permanently changed in an observable way. The transformation you experience affects the way you perceive the world. You come to think about life differently. You discover an aspect of yourself of which you may have been unaware until the point you changed. In the past, you may have assumed that you had a firm grasp of who you are and what you want in life. However, when you experience the power of spiritual transformation, all the things you thought you knew fly right out the window. You feel a much deeper sense of purpose than ever before. You are connected to something greater than you. Put simply, you have grown.

# WISDOM

P O W E R

V I S I O N

# FEELING

**Your metamorphosis can happen in the twinkling of an eye or over a period of time.**[36]

The question is, what exactly triggers this profound transformation? You may have had a series of experiences that caused you to see things differently. Transformation may be a result of a personal crisis. Perhaps your spiritual practices paid off, and you experienced an awakening. Or you may have been dedicated to developing your life. Whatever the case may be, your metamorphosis can happen in the twinkling of an eye or over a period of time. This change touches every aspect of your life. Your thought patterns change. Your emotional baseline changes, too. Even your body can reflect the changes that you have undergone spiritually. It's not a stretch for that to happen because, after all, everything in life springs from the spiritual first.

## Inner Alchemy

Inner alchemy involves learning how to change yourself on the inside so that your exterior world transforms along with you. In the original sense of the word, alchemy is about converting lead into gold. In the context of self-transformation, it is taking your lower nature and elevating it.

As you experience different obstacles and challenges in life, you are given the opportunity to deal with your shadows. Choose to be courageous when you encounter these occurrences. Why? By deciding you will not run away from your shadows, you have a chance to heal your wounds. When you experience deep healing, it leads to inner alchemy. You let go of everything that does not serve you. As a result, you create space in your life for your authentic self to shine.

The transformation process involves bringing together the different aspects of yourself to create a more cohesive being. As you experience the inner spiritual transformation, you learn and grow. Most people live from the Divine Masculine energy and completely neglect the Divine Feminine. However, you have chosen to read this book. By implication, you are learning to integrate both your masculine and feminine sides to achieve wholeness. This is the goal of transformation.

The Black Madonna can help you become more conscious of how you express yourself. She shows you the patterns of behavior that don't serve you. She can show you how you've been holding on to negative emotions and how to release them to become the person you are destined to be. What are some of the ways that the inner alchemical process plays out in your life?

**Purification:** Whenever you lose someone or something dear to you or experience betrayal, you are bombarded with a range of negative emotions. These emotions make it difficult to see the good within that experience. Your mind is clouded by anger. Your heart is weighed down by sadness. There is a sickening feeling in your gut that makes you resent the person who betrayed you or curse life for taking away what you held dear. It is natural to experience these emotions, so do not beat yourself up for not being able to help how you feel. The trouble comes when you don't let go of the negative emotions after acknowledging them. If you hold on too long, they become toxic. How do you purify yourself from this poison? There's no better person to help you with the process than the Black Virgin.

**Refinement:** Give the African Mother free rein to transform your life. You'll discover the trials you deal with can reveal your talents and skills, some of which you had no idea you had. When she walks you through a challenge by taking your hand and giving you courage, the onus is on you to discover your talents and practice to refine them. For instance, your challenge may be that you lost a good-paying job. You feel done for. This circumstance, however, may lead you to discover you are an excellent public speaker. You find you have a way with words. When the Divine Mother inspires you to use that gift, and you do, people begin to gravitate toward you. They want to learn from you. They're happy to pay to hear you speak. You find opportunities that allow you to express these talents even more. You could find yourself in a line of work far more fulfilling than what you lost. This is just one example of how the Black Madonna can help you.

## The Black Madonna: A Catalyst for Change

The archetype of the Black Madonna is the best representation of transformation. She is the embodiment of healing and self-realization. This deity is the representation of nature's dark side. She is the depiction of the unconscious mind and the expression of the feminine principle, unfiltered and unrefined. In her hallowed position as the Mother of everyone, she possesses the power to transform your life and heal you in every way you need. When you invoke the Black Madonna, you draw upon the power of the Divine Feminine, and this power is what transforms your life. How does she help you with your inner alchemy? How does the Black Virgin serve as the catalyst for you to realize your true self and heal?

**She Gives You the Courage to Face Your Shadows.** The first thing the Black Madonna does is to make you aware of your shadow aspect. It is impossible to heal this part of yourself if you don't know it exists to begin with. As her light illuminates your life, you'll discover the dark parts of your psyche and learn what needs to be integrated and healed. These are the parts of yourself you've discarded because the world didn't approve of them. The moment you become aware of your shadow aspect, she helps you learn acceptance. There is a misguided belief that your shadow is something to be repressed or completely ignored. For this reason, many people live a half-life. They literally discard a part of themselves and wonder why they don't feel fulfilled. The Black Virgin helps you accept everything that is you and understand that regardless of your shadow, you are worthy of being loved. The moment you accept her proposal to be at peace with your shadow, you can transform it. She gives you the strength and the courage to bring your wounds to light and heal them. Then, you can integrate your shadow and become whole.

**The Black Madonna Can Help You Live a Life of Authenticity.** One of the ways in which this deity can encourage you to be yourself is to accept your vulnerability. You see, her black skin reflects the fact that you are human. It is a reminder that you struggle just like everyone else. In no way are you alone on your journey. So, there is no reason you should be afraid of your vulnerabilities because everyone has them. If you heed her call to acknowledge that you have vulnerabilities, you can begin to live an authentic life. By working with her, you discover your core values. These values will influence your choices in life and help you live authentically.

**She Connects You with Your Empathetic, Compassionate Self.** Devotees of the Black Virgin can attest that they have more compassion and empathy than before they found her. With her presence in your life, you'll experience the same. You'll realize that everyone has struggles, just as you do. Your empathy grows. Your interactions with the people in your life will become much more meaningful. Why? You deal with others with an open heart, realizing everyone has a burden. So, you treat them a little more kindly, and they give that energy back to you and direct it to others. The world could certainly use a lot more kindness.

**With the Black Virgin, You Can Finally Find Your Purpose.** If you honor the Black Madonna and bring her into every aspect of your life, she will show you your purpose. Could you use some inspiration about what to do with your life? Surrender your affairs to the Black Madonna. It is inevitable that once you do this, you will have a much deeper understanding of why you came to Earth. The more time you spend contemplating the Black Madonna's essence, the more you will feel reassured. Each day, you'll be more certain about your journey, trusting that it is leading you to the perfect end. She is asking you right now to make a bold choice. She wants you to respond to the call of destiny rather than ignore it because you think that's the safer bet. Even if you feel terrified, you can draw strength from her.

# The Power and Impact of the Black Madonna on Your Life

The Black Madonna is the quintessential intercessor. She acts as the middle person between heaven and earth. Whenever you desire something from the spirit world, whether blessing, direction, healing, or wisdom, you can reach out to the Black Madonna and trust that she will deliver on those things. Allow the Black Madonna to play intercessor on your behalf. As you do, you will feel peace that matches nothing else you've ever known. You have someone who can advocate for you and plead your case whenever you are in need. You no longer feel alone by placing your faith fully in the Black Madonna. Once upon a time, you may have been gripped by despair. Now, you know you are always safe.

How can you tell that the Black Mother is interceding on your behalf? You will notice a sense of well-being. Your heart floods with optimism even when you can't see a logical reason to hope. It's as if she pours strength into your spirit. You counter adversity with joy. So, when dealing with a crisis, make it a habit to turn to the Black Madonna.

The Black Virgin has protective powers that affect every aspect of your life when you allow her to be a part of it. Nothing and no one can give you the sense of security that she does. The security she offers is not financial. It does not come in the form of advanced home security systems. She offers you divine security, which is over and above everything else. When you are at your most vulnerable and uncertain, and you worry about who may take advantage of you, she will take care of you.

The Black Virgin protects and provides for every one of her devotees. You can rest in her loving, protective arms in this world full of obstacles and uncertainties. She offers the peace that surpasses all understanding. Are you prone to anxiety? Do you find yourself stressed out all the time? Do you wish you could relax more? In that case, it's about time you asked the Black Madonna to handle your affairs. Once you surrender to her like this, you will handle all the tribulations and trials of life with ease and grace. It wouldn't matter to you if the world were on fire. You would know that amid the chaos, you can find peace with the Mother.

Another power the Black Virgin has is the ability to help you find inner strength. She is a reminder that you can be strong when handling the challenges life throws your way. Some people mistake strength for being aggressive and brash. Often, this is only a show of strength rather than the real deal. It is an illusion meant to hide or camouflage insecurities. What the Black Madonna offers you is more. She shows you true strength, which is a force that endures. It may be quiet, but it is powerful. There isn't a single obstacle that could withstand the strength of the Madonna within you. When you ask her to strengthen you, your doubts and fears may still be there, but you deal with them more confidently. You approach them with tenacity. Sure, you may be in the middle of the most troubling of storms. However, you know you have an indomitable spirit in you in the form of the Black Madonna.

The strength that the Black Virgin offers you is one that you can use in every aspect of life, whether professional or personal. You can use her strength to help you deal with challenging projects with confidence and panache. Are there certain complications and complexities along the path of advancing in your career? Ask her to fill you with her strength. Do you struggle with being authentic and expressing yourself in your personal relationships? She can help you so your emotions and thoughts flow honestly. You'll have no more qualms dealing with conflicts head-on and in the most effective way possible. Whatever your dreams may be, you are no longer timid about making them happen. The Black Madonna's strength encourages you to take risks you ordinarily wouldn't. By trusting in her, your gamble pays off.

## Inspiring Spiritual Change

**Healing and Letting Go:** One thing about the Black Madonna is that she makes it clear it's okay to accept the parts of your life you struggle with. Since everyone has some baggage, she reminds you to avoid letting those things wear you down. Are you serious about growing spiritually? Consider whether you're holding on to old grudges. If you find it tough to bring any to mind, she will remind you of what you have repressed. When you discover these things, you'll see it is essential to let them go. There is no way to progress in your spiritual life when all that negativity weighs you down.

The Divine Feminine is a beacon of light. She shines brightly to show you how to release all the burdens that hold you down. No, she isn't asking you to pretend like your past never happened. If you attempt to lie to yourself about your past, you hold yourself back. Instead, own up to it. When you surrender to her guidance, she will help you understand why you went through what you did. This will be instrumental in helping you release the pain so you can grow. When you realize you no longer have to hold on to the hurt and anger, your life turns around spiritually. This is the gift that the Black Madonna offers you, should you choose to accept it.

**Conquering Fear:** Fear is another thing that can hold you back from spiritual transformation and growth. It's something every human has to contend with. For all the advancements that have been made in science and technology, humanity has yet to crack the code on how to put the kibosh on fear. So, thinking about how to avoid it or totally kill it in your life is unrealistic. There is, however, a solution. You can hand over your fears to the Black Madonna, and she will help you overcome them. It's not like she's going to conduct a spiritual lobotomy that makes it impossible for you to feel fear. Rather, she invites you to face them head-on. It's a daunting thing to do, but if you trust her, you will discover you've always had the courage within you to handle fear.

You can't make spiritual advancements without overcoming fear. Fear is a restrictive energy. It holds you captive. It keeps you from having access to the wonderful opportunities that come your way. Just when you're about to take a leap of faith and do something that would improve your life, fear reminds you of the countless times you failed in the past. So let her help you with that. You're never alone. There's no better companion than the African Mother on your journey. Driven by her power and mystery, you will find the courage to handle everything that gives you nightmares. You see, the Dark Virgin's essence transcends everything you can imagine. Anxiety, worry, fear, and doubt cower in her presence.

**Creative Expression**: Do you find it difficult to develop new ideas? Are you experiencing creative blocks? Did you know the Mother is the best person to help you? Your mother encourages you to trust yourself and your abilities. The Black Madonna does the same thing. She goes a step further, offering you ideas out of this world. The Divine Feminine is a creative force. Remember, it is out of the darkness that all of life emerged. This darkness is embodied in the Black Madonna's dark skin. She serves as a reminder that you, too, can create at every point in time.

Something about acknowledging the Black Madonna's presence in your life makes it possible for you to use your imagination in ways you never thought possible. When you hit a block in your creative work, you are often gripped by fear and a desire to be perfect. By meditating upon the Black Madonna, you receive a reminder from her that you don't need to get it right. You only need to get it done. She also reminds you to check in with yourself to be certain that you are creating what you want to versus what you think others would prefer.

If you want to feel her creative power and action the next time you do some work, consider invoking her presence first. You'll notice that you're taking more risks and having fun expressing yourself authentically. Creation is a deeply spiritual act. It doesn't matter if you're trying to create a feeling within you or a work of art outside of you. You could creatively visualize something in your mind or pour it out onto canvas. Either way, this is a spiritual process. The more you create, the more you are spiritually transformed. You allow her energy to flow through you powerfully, and this will affect every aspect of your life. As you create, you move beyond the ordinary. You translate your inner experiences through your work of art in the most profound and unique ways.

## Inspiring Stories

**Lisa's Story**: Lisa is a very talented artist, but the problem is she never let anyone know it. She was very afraid of being criticized, and because she didn't want to be judged for her art, she never expressed herself how she wanted. Her need for conformity and acceptance would eventually become so bad that it would morph into a desire for perfectionism. Each time she put her paintbrush to her canvas, she could feel the roar of many voices taunting her, even though those voices didn't actually exist. For many years, she remained in her comfort zone and would find that the thing she used to enjoy was no longer fulfilling.

Things would change one day when she found herself visiting a Black Madonna shrine. The first thing she noticed about the shrine was its aura; it felt divine and serene. She would have told you it felt like stepping into an entirely different world if you had asked her. She fixed her eyes on the Black Madonna's striking image and suddenly desired to learn more about her. So, when she returned home, she dove into the topic of the Black Madonna, reading everything she could. She didn't even notice when she fell asleep while researching on the couch.

It turned out this was the intention of the deity. Lisa dreamed of her. The Dark Virgin told her, "Your voice is powerful and unique. Your hands have been blessed to create wondrous works. It is time for you to allow yourself to be as great as you are." Lisa woke up from that dream with the feeling that it was no ordinary dream. she would describe it as being "more real than real life." With a new fire burning passionately in her heart, Lisa went to her studio and immediately got to work. The self-doubt that usually plagued her was no longer there. She dipped her brush into bold and daring colors, creating to her heart's content. The first piece she created after the Black Madonna's vision was unlike anything she'd ever done. She was no longer afraid to put herself out there. Since having that dream, her artistic life has never been the same, both in terms of inspiration and acknowledgment from others.

**Michael's Story**: Michael had a terrible, traumatic childhood. He could remember some of it while he repressed other memories deep into his subconscious. One thing remained undeniable: Michael could feel the weight of all his emotional scars. The trauma tainted everything he did. Imagine having heavy chains around your neck and ankles for over thirty years. He didn't realize he had a date with destiny, specifically with the Black Madonna. On a whim, he decided to accompany a friend on a Black Madonna pilgrimage, even though he thought it was all hogwash. He was only going for the experience to see how this deity deeply enamored others.

Once he arrived, the skeptic in Michael piped up, saying that the people there were a cult. He was about to voice this thought to his friend when he felt a heavy sensation on his chest; without understanding how or why, he felt an intense desire to kneel on the floor. So, he knelt. Yet it was as if the ground was beckoning him, and he couldn't resist. So, he laid down flat. He felt a sense of peace wash over him, the like of which he had never experienced before. The serenity was so great that he wept long and loud. When he would eventually come out of it, he sat for hours in contemplation while the tears continued to flow down his face silently. He had felt the comforting, loving presence of the Black Madonna. He turned to his friend and said, "So, this is what it feels like to be safe?" His friend said nothing but squeezed his hand in comfort and support.

Over the coming days and weeks, Michael would eventually find himself releasing repressed emotions and traumatic memories. It was a challenging process. However, it clearly led to his spiritual transformation. Now, Michael is the sort of man who springs out of bed in the morning as though he's happy to take the day on. There's a lightness in his step that was not there before. He has an easy way about him and is quick to smile. This is the transformative healing power of the Black Madonna in action.

**Emily's Story:** Emily used to be beset with anxiety and stress. It was the reality of her everyday life. She never had a moment to breathe, and when she did, she somehow would find something to fill it with. The thought of sitting still and relaxing made her extremely anxious, to the point where she would bite her nails to the quick. Yet she knew she couldn't stay busy because she was burning out. She knew that her relentless pursuit of perfection could not be sustained and that, at some point, she may burn out permanently. Yet she had no idea how to stop being the way she was.

One day, while in the library researching for work, she felt the calling to take a stroll into the esoteric section. Interestingly, Emily was one of those people you would call a realist. In other words, she didn't care much for religious or spiritual matters. The way Emily saw it, if it was something you couldn't observe with your physical senses, it was not real and did not deserve attention. Imagine her shock and wonder as she found her feet wandering into that aisle of books. She stumbled upon a book about the Black Madonna, and it was as if a voice inside her piped up, saying, "Take that one." So, she took a chance and obeyed.

Emily devoured the book in a matter of hours. She was so enamored by it that she took it home and would reread it. The next day, she did something she had never done her whole life. She called her workplace and told them she would not be available for the next week. According to her, after making that phone call, she felt a peace she had never experienced. She fixed herself a nice cup of tea and sat by her window, looking outside, doing nothing.

Finally, Emily had learned, thanks to the Black Madonna, that her sense of self-worth was not connected to the things she did or accomplished in life. Emily would discover that she's worthy just because – and for no other reason. Her existence alone is a testament to her worthiness. From that point on, Emily was never the same. She had learned how to let go and trust. Interestingly enough, her career took a turn for the better as she decided to rest more and stop to smell the roses more often.

These are only three stories of many demonstrating how the Black Madonna can improve your life on every level. She wants to mother you. She wants to be your friend, to guide and help you. She wants you to know right now that things can be better than you may have imagined or experienced. There is not one thing about you that would exclude you from receiving her blessings and protection. So, take a moment to think about every aspect of your life. Where might you benefit the most from allowing her to have her way with you?

Would you like to develop your spiritual life? Are you tired of seeking for your purpose? Do you wish you could have guidance at every turn? How nice would it be to go through each day knowing you are not alone? What would it be like to live life carefree and trusting as a child does? How great would it be to know you have endless creativity flowing to and through you? Can you imagine what it would be like to have every need met even before you realize you need something?

How freeing is it to know that you can confidently make your choices and trust that the outcomes will be handled by a being who knows all and sees all? How wonderful would it be to find that the relationships you assumed were destroyed forever are now back and better than in the past? Can you picture what it would be like to trust that no matter how it seems, things are always working out for you? What would it be like to know that you have a divine being who rigs life in your favor because she loves you so dearly? What if you could live your life and accomplish far more by resting and trusting than going out to struggle for what you want? All of this is possible if you allow the Black Madonna to be there for you and with you all the way, every day.

However, the Black Madonna does not force herself on you. That would be against the nature of the Divine Feminine. So, right now, she's setting before you an open invitation. It's up to you whether you take it or not. If you want to experience love and power in your life, you have to extend your hand and accept the help she offers. You may find it terrifying. You may feel some doubt or fear. However, you can still accept her help despite those feelings.

# Chapter 5: Her Relation to Mother Goddesses

Did you know that the Black Madonna has connections to Mother Goddesses? She is, after all, the embodiment of motherhood. In this chapter, you'll learn about her connection to the Mother Goddesses across various traditions and cultures. You'll see how she's connected to Isis, Ceres, Cybele, Artemis, Kali, and other goddesses from before Christianity. By looking at the Black Madonna through the lenses of other goddesses who embodied motherhood, you will have an even deeper understanding of what it means to be loved and cherished by the Black Virgin. You will comprehend the different aspects of motherhood and how they can all be found within this one being.

# Isis

Another attribute of this goddess loved by one and all is she is a mother, making her a role model for many women.[87]

Of the many goddesses of ancient Egypt, Isis is one of the most important. Interestingly enough, she used to be obscure because she didn't have temples of her own. However, as the dynastic age continued, more and more people began to acknowledge that she was important. She had a lot of devotees from ancient Egypt and ancient Rome to Afghanistan and England. Even in this day and age, she is honored by pagans.

Isis has a powerful connection with the dead, as she was considered central to all burial rights. She is also strongly connected to life because she is known to be a magical healer who helps the sick and even restores the dead to life. Another attribute of this goddess loved by one and all is she is a mother, making her a role model for many women.

The Egyptian kingship was aware that Isis was important and worth revering. She is depicted as a woman who wears a sheath dress. She also has the horns of a cow on her head, as well as a solar disk. Some of the artistic depictions will also include a hieroglyphic throne. Sometimes, she's depicted as a cow or a sow. Other times, she's seen as a bird or a scorpion. This Mother Goddess is a well-known protector. You could say that she was the precursor to the Black Virgin because the images of the Black Virgin we have today were inspired by images of Isis. Both of them are shown with black or dark skin.

There is much-shared symbolism between Isis and the Black Madonna. By looking at either one, you're looking at a picture of them and seeing stories being crafted through the symbols in their art. If you study ancient Egyptian art depicting Isis, you'll notice an ankh in her hand. That symbol isn't just there to look cool. It is the representation of life itself. It is a sign that she's connected to life and rules the process of rebirth. Now, what about the Black Virgin? You can draw a parallel between her and Isis because she is depicted with a child, representing her connection to life and fertility.

Ancient Egyptians believed that Isis was capable of making miracles happen. In their eyes, she was far more than a goddess to be worshiped. You could always turn to her when you needed healing if you were ill. In fact, so powerful was she that she brought the dead back to life. She offered people hope where there was none. Similar to Isis, the Black Virgin also performs miracles. Once more, the millions who flock to Black Madonna sites worldwide annually don't do so for fun and games. They understand the power that this deity holds. They go, hoping that she can miraculously touch their lives. So, when you think about it, you realize that Isis and Black Madonna carry the same essence of the Divine Feminine.

# Ceres

This myth is the explanation for the seasons and their cycle, as well as a testament to Ceres's power to transform anything and everyone.[88]

In Roman mythology, you have the goddess Ceres. She is responsible for motherly relationships and fertility. Grain crops and agriculture are also her domain. When she's artistically depicted, you'll see her as a woman of mature years, sitting with a crown of wheat stalks, a sheaf of wheat, torches, and a sickle. You can also find her with cereals and a cornucopia full of fruit. This image clearly depicts fertility and growth, showing that this goddess is a provider, able to nurture one and all. This goddess is held in high esteem because she is connected to the cycles of life and death as well as the seasons. She is considered a nurturer, responsible for introducing mankind to agriculture so that they can nurture themselves. Like Isis, she is also a healer and is connected to growth and fertility.

One of the myths of this goddess features her and her daughter Proserpina, who is Persephone in Greek mythology. Cere's daughter was abducted by Hades, also known as Pluto. By taking her daughter away from her, Pluto caused Ceres deep anguish and pain. Deeply aggrieved, Ceres decided she was going to fix things. How? She decided not a single crop would grow on the surface of the Earth until she had her daughter back. Things got so dire that Jupiter had to step in and work something out between Ceres and Pluto regarding Proserpina. So, it was agreed that Proserpina would spend a portion of the year with Hades and the other with Ceres. This myth explains the seasons and their cycle, as well as a testament to Ceres's power to transform anything and everyone.

Now, return your attention to the Black Madonna, and you'll notice that both she and Ceres act as nurturers and protectors. They are both capable of miracles and are intercessors who can intercede on your behalf when you need someone to plead your case. Where the Roman goddess transforms the seasons, the Black Madonna does her own transformation on a spiritual level, changing souls for the better.

# Cybele

She was the caretaker and nurturer of the Earth itself.[89]

This Anatolian goddess is called Mountain Mother. You can trace her origins as far back as the Neolithic times when she was in Çatalhöyük, an Anatolian settlement from 7,500 BC to 6,400 BC and now an official UNESCO World Heritage Site. Now, back to Cybele. This Mother Goddess is responsible for fertility. She was the caretaker and nurturer of the Earth itself. In art, you can find her on a throne with lions resting beside her. Sometimes, other wild animals stand in the lions' places. You can't help but get the sense that she is a force to be reckoned with, swift to protect those who come to her and entrust their lives to her.

Like the Black Virgin, Cybele is a nurturer. They are both mother figures, responsible for ensuring life continues as it has always done. In Greece, Cybele's characteristics would be partially assimilated to aspects of Gaia, who rules the Earth. Ancient Romans knew her as Great Mother or

Magna Mater, which leaves no doubt that she is a nurturer. One of the myths tells of her lover, Attis, going mad and mutilating himself. When he died, Cybele was beside herself. She did all she could and eventually brought him back to life. In this way, she is depicted as being in charge of life, death, and rebirth.

Both Cybele and the Dark Mother share the traits of nurturing and fertility. You can thank them for the cycles of life, the fertility of the land, or any endeavor you execute successfully. What about creativity? Like the Madonna, Cybele influences that aspect of life as well. You can see it in the way she fosters creative energy. Those who worship her use music, dance, and art in her honor.

## Artemis

This goddess reigns supreme over the moon, the wilderness, and the hunt.[40]

Artemis is a goddess worthy of honor and respect. She is the daughter of Leto and Zeus and Apollo's twin. Imagine being transported to Ancient Greece, where you could witness the awe and reverence with which the people honored her. This goddess reigns supreme over the moon, the wilderness, and the hunt. She is usually depicted with hunting knives, a bow, and a quiver full of arrows. Of all the animals and plants there are, she is partial to deer and cypress trees. Undoubtedly, her love for and connection to nature are apparent. For this reason, the Black Madonna has the same love for nature, and some artwork shows her surrounded by lush greenery or other symbols of nature.

By studying Artemis and the Dark Virgin, you'll notice their parallels, archetypally speaking, as they are both nurturers. She's known for taking care of young girls, in particular, keeping them safe. Another interesting parallel is in the aspect of fertility. The Grecian goddess oversees all matters pertaining to midwifery and childbirth, which shows you she's connected to life, fertility, and the cycles that rule one and all.

The Black Madonna and Artemis are known for their association with the moon, the mysteries of the feminine, and wild energy. Sometimes, you'll find the Black Madonna standing confidently on the crescent moon, embodying wildness and the unconscious. Some similarities exist even when it comes to the legends and myths surrounding both of these beings. One of the legends tells of Artemis helping Leto, her mother, so she could birth her twin, Apollo, with ease. Another myth discusses how Artemis kept Leto safe from Hera, Zeus's jealous wife. These stories demonstrate her powerful, benevolent, and protective nature. These traits of Artemis can be found in the Dark Mother, too.

Women turn to Artemis when they need help dealing with the painful experience of childbirth, and she comes through for them. So, like the Dark Virgin, Artemis also performs miracles and swiftly answers sincere prayers. Artemis is also a virgin, like the Dark Madonna. She didn't care for male attention. Her attendants were also expected to remain chaste, and when they broke their chastity vow, they would suffer the consequences. These beings are the epitome of motherhood, godhood, feminine strength, and nature.

# Kali

Time, creation, and change are all in her hands, and so are death and destruction, which is why devotees know she's not to be trifled with.⁴

Kali is a Hindu goddess who is loved and feared by many, and for good reason. Her power is exceedingly great. Time, creation, and change are all in her hands, and so are death and destruction, which is why devotees know she's not to be trifled with. You see, in Hindu tantric tradition, there are ten Mahavidyas. The word *Mahavidya* means "Great Wisdoms," and they are a group of ten goddesses, including Tara, Tripura Sundari, Bhuvaneshwari, Chhinnamasta, Bhairavi, Baglamukhi, Matangi, Dhumavati, Kamala, and Kali. The first time Kali made herself known to the world was when she manifested from Durga. Her goal was simple: To end all that is evil so that those who are innocent can be free from its terrors. She would come to be known as the Mother of the Universe and the Divine Mother by sects devoted to her.

Interestingly enough, the Black Mother is also called the Queen of the Earth and the Queen of Heaven since she is the transcendent version of the Virgin Mary. On top of that, she represents the Immaculate Conception and incorruptibility. This shows both beings are the same in their opposition to all that is evil and corrupt. The Black Madonna has never given herself over to a man or male deity, nor will she ever.

This Dark Virgin is a protector, similar to Kali, as the latter offers a safe haven for those who trust her. She gives them true liberation.

Mythologically speaking, the Black Madonna and Kali the Destroyer share certain interesting traits. Consider *Sara-la-Kâli*, also known as "Sarah the Black One." Many believe she shares a connection with the Black Mother and will often speak of her in that context. She is honored by gypsies, who see her as their royal ruler, and Catholics. You may wonder what the connection is between Sarala-Kâli and the goddess Kali. Well, this being is the patron saint of the Romani people who originate from India. In case you wondered why she has an English name, in Romani, she is *Sara e Kali*. Sarah or Sara is etymologically Hebrew, meaning "noblewoman" or "princess." Not only that, but you can also find the name *Sara* within the Durga Saptashati, which is an ancient Hindu scripture dedicated to Durga, the Divine Mother herself. In this sacred, ancient text, Durga is called Kali, as well as Sara.

In the Durga Saptashati, you'll find stories of Durga fighting demons who possessed great power, which they used to cause chaos and terrorize the world. The goddess would morph from one form to another to defeat these powerful entities. These stories show how she, like the Dark Mother, fights your battles to protect you from anything and anyone seeking to harm you.

## Ala

Ala is a deity of the Igbo tribe in Eastern Nigeria. Her devotees also call her Ali, Ale, Ana, or Ani, depending on the Igbo dialect they speak. Her name literally means "ground," a reference to the extent of her power. Creativity, fertility, morality, and the Earth are her domains, over which she rules gracefully. She also oversees the affairs of the underworld. Like a pregnant woman, she carries the souls of ancestors and the dead in her womb. You can infer that she not only rules the Earth but *is the Earth herself*. She ensures everyone acts justly and fairly, following the rules of the land. Like the Black Madonna, she is known for fertility and is a protector and nurturer. She is also seen as the goddess of love, full of compassion and wisdom.

Ala is depicted as a deity with a regal aura, often with her family around her while she sits on her throne. This is reminiscent of the Black Madonna and her little one, demonstrating motherhood. Her devotees know that when they pray to her, much like the Black Madonna, she answers with a miracle.

## Oya

Oya is a Goddess from Western Nigeria. She is also called Yansä in Latin America, where she is known and revered. An orisha, she is in control of violent storms, bringing wind and lightning wherever she sees fit. She's also a river goddess; her devotees see her as overseeing children. Many who have been barren have received the miracle of conception from her as she blessed and continues to bless those who ask with children. Unlike the Black Madonna, she did get married to Sango, the god of thunder. However, they're both known for being nurturing and protective of those they know belong to them. Oya is known for protecting her people from their enemies and any injustice toward them. This is similar to the Black Madonna, who has been known to protect her people from those who sought to oppress them. These deities are also known to cause renewal and radical change as needed. Oya does this through her winds, which can both create and destroy.

## In Conclusion

Having read through all the mythologies of these different goddesses across cultures and traditions, it should be obvious that the Black Madonna is the embodiment of the Divine Feminine. From the dawn of time, humanity has been aware of this being or energy. She has gone by multiple names, but now you know her as the Black Madonna. Having read this chapter, it should be difficult to deny the interconnectedness of the Dark Virgin with other mother goddesses from various cultures and times.

Before Christianity, many people had unique beliefs and deities they trusted. These beings shared deep connections with nature and the cycles of life. Among them, you had those with the Mother Goddess archetype. Evidently, beliefs evolve with time. So, when Christianity rose, it strongly influenced how people interacted with spiritual matters. The Christian missionaries did all they could to spread their way of interacting with the divine far and wide. Sometimes, that meant looking for parallels between Christian tenets and the elements that made up the traditional religious beliefs of the people they hoped to convert. It was much easier to convince people to become Christians by helping them see how their present beliefs paralleled the Christian faith. Some say this is how the earth goddesses of old would eventually become the Black Madonna. Regardless of what happened, the fact remains she serves as a bridge to connect all beliefs. Within her dark skin, you can find the unification of all spiritual truths. This esoteric theory should make it clear how and why the Black Madonna has so many similarities with the ancient Mother Goddesses that you have learned about. In the next chapter, you will learn more esoteric interpretations of this mysterious being.

# Chapter 6: Esoteric Interpretations

The Black Madonna is associated with divine mysteries and esoteric aspects of spirituality. In this chapter, you will learn about this deity's esoteric and mystical interpretations. As you already know, she is full of symbolism. The question is, what do these symbols mean? How can you make them more personal to you? The way to reap the rewards of her symbolism is through understanding them. Therefore, The first step will be to explain what esotericism is and why it is important when studying spirituality.

## Understand Esotericism

Esotericism is about diving into knowledge to discover deeper meaning, which is often hidden and difficult to spot at first glance. There are certain practices and beliefs which only a few people understand on a deep level. You may be looking at a religious text or considering a particular deity and not immediately notice the deeper layers of meaning to them. Why? These esoteric aspects of a belief or religion are meant to take time to grasp. They require deep contemplation and reflection.

The word "esoteric" is etymologically rooted in esôterikos, a Greek word that means "within" or "inner." This is not your average kind of knowledge. For the most part, people only have knowledge that is publicly available or exoteric. However, when you know something esoterically, it means you have come to discover the truth of that thing from within yourself. When you think of the esoteric, you can think of things like the occult, mysticism, and spirituality. All of these things serve to help you have a better understanding of how life works and your place in it.

Several principles govern esotericism. Before considering the esoteric nature of the Black Madonna, you should understand what these principles are about.

**The Principle of Hidden Knowledge:** Esoteric knowledge is never publicly available. Usually, this information is shared between the master, who has come to understand the spiritual subjects, and the students, who seek to learn. So, people will journey to ashrams, shrines, or other sacred places, hoping to receive esoteric knowledge from those in the know. Esoteric knowledge requires secrecy. Not everyone gets to understand it. This is because only some are prepared to handle the power that comes with esoteric knowledge. Some people may not know what to do with it, while others may use the knowledge for nefarious intentions. This is why esoteric knowledge is only given to a select few. A second reason for this selectivity is to prevent the message from being diluted or corrupted in some way. All esoteric knowledge is profound and sacred. When you truly understand how the universe works, it makes you a powerful person. What you do with that power is another matter entirely. This is why the keepers of esoteric knowledge jealously guard what they know. These people have the responsibility of safeguarding wisdom that is timeless and ancient.

**The Principle of Spiritual Evolution:** The evolution of the human spirit is another principle behind esoteric knowledge. Everyone has the ability to experience personal growth and achieve true transformation from within, which then leads to them being enlightened. You are no exception. The truly esoteric person understands that it is possible to develop spiritually – but also *necessary*. Only when you consciously develop your spiritual journey can you experience deeper self-awareness and access states of consciousness higher than you are accustomed to.

The truly esoteric person understands that it is not only possible to develop spiritually but also necessary.⁴⁸

Your soul is on a journey. As it goes down its path, it must evolve. When you understand the esoteric and live your life according to its principles, you will go beyond regular everyday experiences. Things that used to bother you deeply will no longer be a problem because you can see past what your reality is showing you.

The first step to becoming spiritually developed is realizing you have an ego. The ego consists of all the stories you've told yourself. It is everything you believe to be true about yourself. The moment you realize you are far more than your ego, you evolve past these limiting stories and beliefs you have. You see how your ego is not your true self but a tool to be used by your soul to experience life. Therefore, to practice esotericism, you need to be willing to self-reflect to become more aware of your authentic nature. You'd be hard-pressed to find a better way to do this than through mindfulness and meditation on the Black Madonna and her essence.

**The Principle of Symbolism and Allegory:** Every esoteric tradition understands and accepts that symbolism and allegory are important. Words can only do so much to transmit meaning so that you can truly understand the topic. However, symbolism is an excellent way to get the meaning of an idea deep into your soul. The same can be said for allegories. As a human being, you naturally tend to pay attention to stories.

You could argue your everyday existence is full of stories. Every person is a walking book full of stories, too. The classic three-act structure is one that humans resonate with because everyone is wired to understand stories. So, what better ways would there be to encapsulate the deeper meanings of esoteric concepts than through stories?

Understand that symbols are far more than simple representations of ideas. Think of each one as a doorway or a portal that allows you access to a deeper and even more real version of reality than you've ever known. Symbols and allegories cut through the mundane and ordinary, allowing you to reach deep into the heart of the archetypes that make up life. In esotericism, each symbol carries far more meaning than you can glean when you are first introduced to it. Through regular contemplation and meditation upon the symbol, you find yourself peeling back the layers to discover even richer meanings. Think of it like a tree trunk with concentric circles, except in esotericism, the circles never end.

**The Principle of Divine Connection:** Esotericism implies that you are connected to divinity. Unlike other traditional religious systems, Esotericism shows you do not need an intermediary to access spiritual powers or enlightenment. You have the power to transform yourself, and you can do so without any help. Traditional religion insists that you must go through some intermediary. In those rigid structures, there is a need for hierarchy. This can be rather limiting to the psyche and soul. Therefore, esotericism is a liberator. It helps you break the traditional religious chains that hold you back and allows you direct access to the divine source that created you.

The beautiful thing about being an esotericist is you know you can contact the source or creator of all things. You know you aren't limited by your background or what you believe in terms of religion. You know the divine does not care where you stand in society. You deeply understand that your connection to divinity supersedes every possible limitation that people can come up with. Sure, you may belong to a certain religious group. You may take part in certain religious activities. However, you are also aware of the freedom you have to get in touch with the source of life directly.

**The Principle of Holistic Understanding:** As an esotericist, you realize that life can be understood on a holistic level. It is tough to deny the interconnectedness of concepts, ideas, and all created things. The more aware you become of yourself and how the universe works by diving deeper into esoteric knowledge, the more you will notice the profound connections between seemingly unrelated things. This is the principle of holistic understanding, where you can learn the truth about life, from how a butterfly flies to how marketers entice people to purchase a product.

The true esotericist understands that there are connections between the physical and spiritual world, even if they may not be immediately apparent. They know the created world is simply the microcosm of the macrocosm. Look around you. If you pay close attention and truly ponder it, you will notice that everything around you is a reflection of a deeper spiritual force or principle. Whether you look at life through the lens of mysticism, astrology, alchemy, or anything else, you will notice it's all interwoven. Every field of study is part of the puzzle that makes up existence. As an esotericist, it is your job to find the thread that connects all these things and to use what you learn from the connections to develop your soul. You learn the importance of seeing beyond the superficial. You never make the mistake of assuming that something is irrelevant. As a result, you can find patterns in everything. Perceiving and understanding the patterns is key to developing your life spiritually and in every other aspect.

## The Esoteric Origins of the Black Madonna

Now that you understand the fundamental principles of esotericism, it is time to discover why it should be a key part of approaching your relationship with the Black Madonna. However, before getting into that, here is a close look at the esoteric origins of the Black Madonna.

**The Unification of All Ancient Earth Goddesses:** In a previous chapter, you discovered how the Black Madonna shares ties with ancient Earth goddesses. Humanity has always been aware of the Divine Feminine, so the feminine deity has always been worshiped. Since the dawn of time, humanity has been aware of the energy that drives the cycles of life. People are drawn by the desire to honor this energy, which is responsible for the abundance and fertility that everyone enjoys. People from prehistoric times would worship an Earth goddess representing this feminine force. They understood that when it came to being nurtured and protected, they owed their thanks to this force.

So, the Black Madonna, with her dark skin, represents this archetype from ancient times. Her dark skin is reminiscent of the Earth, with its rich, fertile soil, which is responsible for allowing food to grow and sustaining all of life. So, esoterically speaking, the Black Madonna is a connection between the sacredness of Mother Earth and all the mysteries surrounding the creation process.

**The Mystery of Alchemy:** Next, there's the matter of the connection between the Black Madonna and alchemy, a process that involves turning base metals into gold. Some say this process is only figurative, while others believe there are actual alchemists who successfully transformed base metals into gold. Either way, the transformation process happens within you. Somewhere along the line, there is a point where you no longer exist the way you've always known yourself. Some people call this ego death, while in alchemy, it is known as the *nigredo*. This is a stage of darkness. Everything you thought you knew about who you are is suddenly dissolved. This is another esoteric interpretation of the dark skin of the Madonna. However, from the darkness emerges the gold you carry within you. What is this gold in the spiritual context? It is your enlightenment.

**The Mystery Schools and Their Initiation Rites:** Remember, one of the tenets of esotericism is the fact that it is selective and secret. For the longest time, there have been different mystery schools that only allow those who qualify for initiation access to the knowledge they carry. The Black Madonna herself is an enigma. Her mystery finds its roots in the ancient traditions. Those who attended ancient mystery schools to learn more about her realized she embodies inner transformation. They knew she alone carries true spiritual insights that radically transform and empower you. They did not share this information with the masses but kept it for those who truly seek deep experiences with the Black Madonna. Think of her esoterically as the portal to spiritual insight and truth. She makes it so you don't have to find an ancient mystery school. Instead, you can come to her with an open heart and seek the light of her wisdom.

**Hermetic and Gnostic Touches:** Hermetic and Gnostic traditions are well known for encouraging you to experience inner illumination and deepen your spiritual practice. With deep study, you will notice the connection between the Black Madonna and Hermetic and Gnostic values. For one thing, the color black is not seen as a devilish or evil thing. It is understood under these principles that there is so much more to black than darkness and negativity. Instead, in Hermeticism and Gnosticism, black is seen as the material from which all of life emerges. It is understood that all spiritual insight comes from darkness.

# The Alchemy of the Soul

The first stage of soul alchemy involves the blackening, where everything dissolves into utter chaos. Your consciousness feels like it has descended into darkness. This is *nigredo*, where you finally face the shadow self you've been avoiding your whole life. You realize there is no way out than to go through the challenge you are dealing with. The blackness of the Dark Virgin is representative of this stage of alchemy. She represents what it means to go through the dark night of the soul.

Next comes the albedo. When experiencing this stage of alchemy, it feels as if someone cracked a window and let some light in. You feel as if you are being purified. Little by little, you gain more clarity about what you should do in life and feel enlightened. The Black Madonna symbolizes the duality of life. She carries within her both darkness and light. So, this stage of the alchemy of your soul represents the light essence of the Madonna.

Finally, you experience the *rubedo*. This final alchemical stage refers to the transformation of your soul. At this point, you realize that you were never separate from divinity. You only perceived yourself to be that way. When you get to this stage of transformation, you find yourself expressing the transcendent nature of the Black Madonna. You experience what it means to be connected to heaven and earth. This is the point where you finally realize that there is no way anyone could separate you from the love of the Creator.

There is an extra element to the alchemical transformation of your soul. It is the realization that you will always carry within you both your light and dark aspects. Some assume enlightenment means they will never relapse into a place of darkness. However, there will always be new levels of enlightenment to attain. Each time, you will experience something akin to the darkness of the soul. When you accept this, your dark knights are far easier to handle. You no longer allow yourself to wallow as you did in the past, and in fact, you become excited because you know your breakthrough will be beyond anything you've ever imagined possible for yourself.

It is terrible to experience the dark night of the soul, thinking there is no one to support you. However, when you become aware of the Black Madonna and this period hits you, it's comforting to know she has your back. She is a steadfast and true friend, a companion who will never abandon you, no matter how ugly things may seem. This is what you are experiencing right now. Dare to surrender yourself to her. Dare to trust that she will help you find the enlightenment you need to pull yourself out of the hole you are in. Dare to trust that the darkness is not permanent, and eventually, the sun will rise in your life again.

## The Cosmic Cycle

Esoterically, the Black Madonna is a dance of rhythms. You find up and down within her, high and low, ebb and flow. One of the rhythms in this being is darkness and creation. The Madonna represents the primordial darkness from which everything created in the world comes. When you think about darkness, what comes to your mind? Do you assume it is the absence of light? This is not the sort of darkness being referred to here in the context of the Black Madonna's esoteric interpretation.

The African Mother's darkness is a powerful and creative one. It is the womb of all things and beings in existence and to exist. It is the same womb where you can expect your soul to be transformed for good. This black color, which the Black Madonna carries, represents the cosmic void unrestricted by time. This same void births and carries the galaxies and stars you see. The darkness draws you, asking you to plunge into the depths of your spiritual aspects and see what gold you can emerge with.

There is also a dance between the Divine Feminine and the Divine Masculine. As already explained, the Black Madonna epitomizes the feminine principle. However, there is a need for balance in your spiritual life, which is why the Divine Masculine is a necessary counterpart. At first glance, it may not seem like it, but the Black Madonna has symbolism that shows the essential nature of the Divine Masculine. You see, she has a strong connection to the Earth and is connected to light and darkness. Since she represents cycles and rhythms, it only makes sense that she also carries within her the Divine Masculine, an active force that is necessary for transformation. To sum it all up, the Black Madonna is responsible for integrating opposites. This is a reminder that you must discover the dual natures within yourself and accept them as valid.

# The Rewards of the Exploring the Black Madonna's Esotericism

**You Will Realize the Depth of Symbolism** When you approach your study and understanding of the Black Madonna with esotericism. You will discover a symbolic depth to this deity. Think about her dark skin, for instance. What else could you glean from the information you have received from this book about what her skin represents? If you want more information on the symbolism of her dark skin, it would be best for you to meditate on it. When you spend time deeply contemplating the Black Madonna's dark skin, you will receive levels of knowledge and insight that others may not have. What's the best part? The information you receive will be unique to you and your life experience. So, it would be in your best interest to begin thinking of the Black Madonna from an esoteric point of view. If you ever feel stuck when trying to understand a certain aspect of this being, you can ask her for help. She will gladly help you discover useful insights.

**You Will Discover New Depths of Connection to Her.** You use esoteric practices like prayer and meditation to connect with the Black Madonna. You will discover the depth of the connection you share with the divine. Like it or not, you are always connected to your source. You only think you are not because you have not allowed yourself to see it. So, an interesting thing starts to happen when you meditate upon the Black Madonna's image or essence, pray to her, or contemplate what she means to you. You approach everything from the mundane to the most important, from a spiritual place. With constant esoteric practices to connect you to the Black Madonna, you receive deep spiritual insights that you've never had before. These insights will open up within you and give you a profound understanding you could never receive from any book or guru out there. Books, videos, gurus, teachers, and whatever else in the exterior world can only teach you so much. However, you will achieve true transformation when you decide you desire esoteric knowledge concerning the Black Madonna.

**You Will be Reborn and Transformed into a More Transcendent Version of Yourself.** Once more, the Black Madonna is known for her power over rebirth and transformation. You already know the core tenets of esotericism, which include personal development and spiritual growth. When you work with the Black Madonna and seek esoteric knowledge, you will undoubtedly become different. As she gives you new insight, you will begin to think, speak, and act through that filter. For instance, if you are a workaholic, and the Dark Virgin reveals the essence of rest and allowing things to manifest on their own, you may begin to take things easy and seek more time to relax. With your new appreciation for rest and relaxation, you may notice even how you walk is different. You take deeper breaths. You stop trying to rush things. You understand that everything happens in its own time. As a result, the people who have always known you may find that you are a completely different person. You also will attest to the fact that you feel different now. You start prioritizing ease and flow over struggle and strife. You wonder how it is that you could have ever lived any other way. You realize that resting and choosing ease and flow allows even greater abundance in life and more progress regarding your career. Eventually, it occurs to you that your old self is dead. You have experienced true transformation. You are reborn.

# Chapter 7: Connecting with the Black Madonna

You're still reading this book, which further affirms that you really are drawn to the Black Madonna. She beckons you, asking you to give life with her a try. However, before you commit fully and take the plunge, it's worth asking yourself what you hope to experience by having her in your life. What motive do you have for wanting to connect with the Divine Mother? If you can answer this question clearly and sincerely, you're going to experience what you seek and then some.

## Answering the Virgin's Call: Growing Inner Resonance

So, you want to understand why you're connecting with the Black Virgin, which means you need time and space to reflect. You must be intentional about it whenever you are ready to do this. Pick a time you'll use for this exercise. The room you're in should be quiet and comfortable. Adjust the lighting so it's ambient rather than harsh. If you can't find some quiet because of others around you, you may want to do this exercise when everyone else is asleep. Alternatively, you could use a white noise machine or play white noise on the internet using your headphones or speakers to drown out the noise around you. You're about to get in touch with yourself, so you want it to be just you with your thoughts, no distractions, no interruptions.

So, you want to understand why you're connecting with the Black Virgin, which means you need time and space to reflect."

**Openness**: You have to start with an open mind. Have no expectations about how or when the Black Virgin will answer you. *Trust that she will.* Trust that when she answers, whether during this exercise or some other day, you'll know it without a doubt. Now, shut your eyes and breathe deeply. Allow your heart to be open. You're doing this with a curious, exploring mind that seeks to learn, not one that's convinced it knows all there is to know. If you start with this attitude, you'll surely discover what your motives are.

**Reflection**: Now, it's time to reflect on what about the Black Virgin draws you to her. Do you love the fact that she's an enigma? Perhaps you know she has so many secrets and profound insights to share with you, and you're excited to put them into practice in your life. Is there a certain esoteric truth about her that calls you? Do you love that she so effortlessly embodies light and darkness without elevating one over the other? Could it be that you enjoy the thought of the peace she offers your heart, mind, and soul? Are you seeking release from pain and suffering that has become difficult to bear? The only way to know what you seek is to ask yourself questions like these. You could consider the aspects of your life you feel dissatisfied with. If you're unhappy with every part of your life, that's okay too. There's nothing too big or too small for the Black Madonna to help you with. Be candid with yourself as you ask these questions. You may speak with yourself aloud or in your mind. For best results, you should use a journal because you'll have something to refer to later on, and you'll be glad to note how your motives to connect with the Mother evolve.

**Emotions:** During this self-reflection exercise, you may notice interesting emotions bubbling to the surface. You could feel anything from restless longing to comfort as you think about her. Trust that whatever emotion bubbles up is supposed to be there. If you ask yourself, "Why do I feel this way right now?" and sit with the question, you will discover interesting insights. The answers will clue you in on why you want to connect with the Black Virgin. Let them flow onto the page of your journal, holding nothing back. The Black Virgin does not judge you for your feelings or thoughts, so you don't have to worry about putting on a show of holiness and piety. Write your feelings, raw and unfiltered. Let it all flow.

**The Past:** It's time to dive into your past. This portion of the exercise isn't meant to make you feel regret, shame, pain, or judge yourself negatively. You're combing through your past for experiences that resonate with the Black Virgin's essence and symbolism. You're looking for times when she may have shown up for you, but you weren't aware it was her. Recall the darkest, lowest points in your life. You know them. Those were times when you were desperate for guidance, longing for a healing touch, thirsty for change but unsure how to make it happen. Look for signs the Black Virgin was with you, and if you can't think of any, turn your attention to how she could have been a great comfort and help if you knew you could call upon her and receive miracles.

**Release:** Digging through your past is uncomfortable. You may find yourself caught in the throes of the negativity, anger, hurt, shame, and heaviness that gripped you. This is a good thing. It's an opportunity for you to release those emotions. Do not judge them or the experiences that led to them as terrible. Instead, welcome the feelings that flood your mind and body. Sit with them, and allow them to lead you. You may find your writing gets more frantic and erratic. Perhaps you have the urge to scream or cry. Do that. Don't bottle anything in. What you're doing right now is choosing to accept every aspect of yourself, and that includes the part of you that suffered and probably is still in pain.

**Clarity:** Now, turn your attention to what you'd like to experience by becoming one with the African Mother and making her a real presence in your life. You'll have some answers come to mind at this point. Write them down, then continue to drill past the surface by asking why. "Why do I want that?" When you get an answer, ask the question again. Continue until you drill down to the core of what your soul hungers for. When you know how you'd like the Black Mother to feed you, allowing her to satisfy you becomes easier when you officially welcome her into your life.

## A Deeper Connection: Inner Resonance and Intuition

You may know many people who profess a certain faith, but for whatever reason, you can tell their connection to it isn't strong. They don't take it seriously. They're religious or spiritual on paper, and that's about it. Well, you're going to avoid making the same mistake they do. If you want to make this work, you must be in touch with your intuition. Everyone has intuition. If you split the words, you get "in" and "tuition." This is teaching, wisdom, and guidance that comes from within you. The odds are you're an intuitive person, seeing as you've been drawn to this book. However, if you get the sense that you could develop your intuition further, you should. You see, you need that inner guidance to help you understand your true self and your motives for desiring the Mother's healing heart and loving light in your life.

So, what is inner resonance? How does that help you connect with the Black Mother on a deep level? Think about your favorite song. If you can, listen to it right now. As it plays, notice the way you feel. If it's a happy song, you feel your mood lift. If it's a sad song, you feel your mood shift to reflect that sadness, or if you were already sad before listening, you will feel your sadness deepen. That's how inner resonance works. It is what you experience when you feel something on a level so deep, it's soul-deep. So, when you initiate contact with the Black Virgin, you'll notice the same thing. It's like there's a force tugging on your soul. You may not have the words to describe your experience, but it will feel like you know her. It will appear you've become one with her, and you "get" her. Her thoughts and emotions become yours. You find unity between your mind and the symbolism of the Mother. This is pure resonance.

Now, return to the matter of your intuition. Your intuition will confirm that the resonance you feel is real. It lets you know you are in the presence of the Divine Feminine herself. Your intuition could be a gentle voice on the inside. It could feel like a strong knowing. It will often show up using the language of feelings. The further you go on your journey with the Black Virgin, the stronger your intuition will become, and the deeper your connection with her will be. So, listen to your inner voice. It knows where you should go. If you allow it, you'll feel guided. It's like an invisible hand on your shoulder; its touch is gentle as it steers you down the right path. It could feel like an urge to learn even more than you have about the Dark Mother. It could be a desire to shut your doors, shut your eyes, and sit quietly contemplating her grace and love. Whatever it is you're feeling, trust it. Intuition is your soul speaking to you through the language of your feelings.

## Developing Stronger Intuition

You now understand intuition is important, and it would only serve you to get better at using it. So, what practical ways can you strengthen your intuitive muscles?

**Try Meditation.** How? Meditation is a mindfulness practice where you focus on one thing for some time and nothing else. Typically, meditators focus on their breath or some other steady sound. You could do this or get a picture or some other visual representation of the Black Virgin and keep your attention on her. When your mind wanders away from whatever you have chosen to focus on, gently return your attention where it belongs. Beating yourself up about losing focus is a waste of time and will set you back. Meditation is mastering your attention and awareness, and the fact that you keep noticing you've been distracted is good for you. With time and practice, you'll find the moments of distraction decrease. People who have meditated for years even develop the ability to meditate in the chaos of busy traffic. However, you need time to get to this point. You will only enjoy the benefits of meditation if you practice every day. So, set aside five to ten minutes when you can sit in silence to meditate. With time, you can increase the duration of your sessions.

**Journal Daily.** When you journal, you're getting in touch with yourself. You're checking in, seeking where you're at relative to where you've been. You're engaged in a dialogue with yourself, using the medium of paper. Your journal should contain the events of the day, how you feel about them, how you feel about yourself, your spiritual journey, insights you receive from within, intuitive messages, dreams, patterns you've noticed, and anything else that comes to mind. By journaling, you strengthen the connection between your mind and soul, making it easier to pick up on intuitive messages and tell them apart from random thoughts.

**Spend Time in Nature.** Nature is an excellent tool to help you become a more intuitive person. You could be up in the mountains, deep in the heart of the forest, or by a babbling brook. It doesn't matter, as long as you're surrounded by nature. When you're in natural settings, it does wonders for your intuition. You're removed from the daily stresses and chaos that demand your attention. Instead, you're in Mother Nature's presence. You're sitting with the Black Virgin herself. The more time you spend in her energy in nature, the better you'll be at hearing her call and responding.

Nature is an excellent tool to help you become a more intuitive person."

**Pay Attention to Your Dreams.** There's no better medium for your soul or the spirit world to reach you than through your dreams. So, keep a dream journal. When you wake, don't be in a hurry to open your eyes and roll out of bed. Don't move. Remain where you are, and allow the last image from your dream to come to you. Then, you can work your way backward. When you've remembered it all, you can then journal. If you get up too fast, move around too much, or allow your mind to begin its habitual worrying and planning for the day, you may forget your dreams.

If you are one of those people who can't recall their dreams, or you think you don't dream, what do you do? Remain in bed, eyes shut, body still and relaxed, and pay attention to how you feel. Sit with the feeling, and then write that in your journal. Don't be surprised when you start remembering your dreams. The more you journal them, the easier it will be to recall them because you've taught your subconscious mind that it is important to remember your dreams. So, it will facilitate your dream recall.

**Notice What Your Body Is Doing.** Sometimes, you'll get an intuitive feeling so strong you feel it in your body. Your body has wisdom. It is wiser than you realize. So, whenever you need to make a decision, notice the way you feel. Is there some tightness or heaviness in your chest? That could tell you there's something wrong with the option you've selected. Do you feel light in your chest? Is your breathing deep and sure? The odds are you've chosen the best path for you at this time, so you should proceed with your decision and trust it. Some people get an instant headache or tummy ache when they meet people who are no good. Is this you? Recall instances when you had to make a critical decision. Think back to when you first met someone who wound up being toxic. Remember when you met the people you feel most at home with? Can you recall how those experiences went? Can you reenact them in your mind and pay attention to the feeling you get in your body? This is how to master your body's intuitive signals.

**Decide to Trust Your Intuition.** Some people receive intuitive messages, but they dismiss them as nothing-burgers. They don't act on what they get. When you ignore the messages from within, you weaken your ability to perceive them. The same thing happens when you doubt what you're being told. So, decide to trust your gut, regardless of how it plays out. Whenever you get a strong feeling or are nudged to do something, follow through with no questions asked and no expectations. You will be tempted to "logic" your way out of acting. However, you must accept that logic is severely limited when it comes to matters of the spirit. You cannot attempt to contain the unspeakable, unimaginable vastness of spirit in the small, rigid cage of logic. Otherwise, you'll not only be unable to sense when your intuition is telling you something, but you'll also live a needlessly difficult life.

Whichever route you choose to help you develop your intuition, you should be patient with yourself. This development will take time. Suppose you attempt to rush the process or get upset with yourself for not seeing results sooner. In that case, you'll only slow your progress or stop it altogether.

## A Guided Meditation Practice

Guided meditation is similar to meditation, except your attention will be on what your guide says. You'll be asked to visualize or feel things. If you worry you can't visualize, understand it's no different than imagining something in your mind. Some people can use all their senses in their imagination with no problem, while others may be better at feeling, hearing, or something else. Whatever the case is for you, you can still work with this guided meditation by imagining it is true, even if your inner visuals or other senses aren't that clear.

**Starting Out:** You need to be somewhere peaceful. If other people are around you, ask them to leave you alone for the next ten to fifteen minutes. Turn off all your devices, as you want to avoid being dragged out of this meditation by an inconvenient notification. Wear comfortable clothing that doesn't itch or feel too tight, and sit or lie comfortably. Place your feet flat on the floor if you're sitting on a chair. Your back should be straight, but not uncomfortably so. Picture a wire that's connected to the top of your head. Imagine someone pulling it, causing you to straighten your posture. If you're sitting on the floor, you may sit in an easy lotus position. You could also sit with your feet stretched out in front or in any other position that will allow you to relax. Shut your eyes and begin breathing deeply. As you breathe, allow your mind to quieten and let your body relax. Remember your intention; you want to invite the Black Madonna into your space and your life.

**Visualizing:** Picture yourself in a forest. The greens are vibrant, the sounds are pleasant, and the aura of that space is one of tranquility. You love being here. You enjoy watching the warm, golden sun dancing on the floor as it comes through the leaves being rustled by the wind, which feels delicious on your skin. You feel drawn to look up ahead of you and give in to the urge. As you do, you sense the Black Madonna's presence. She's not far now. She can't be. She's the reason this sacred space exists.

You walk further down the forest path, which is strewn with brown leaves on either side. Some of those leaves are on the path, too. They crinkle and crunch beneath your feet, adding to the sense of serenity and sacredness of the forest. You come to a stop when you see a female figure before you. Her form is adorned with a robe that flows elegantly. Her face is the picture of peace and serenity. You look in her eyes, twin dark orbs full of ancient wisdom and the knowledge of things too wondrous to capture with words. You notice her skin is dark. It's like it whispers to you that it carries the deepest of mysteries. It tells you it nurtures the cosmos and can nurture you, too. This being is the Black Madonna.

**Making the Connection**: Now, allow yourself to feel her energy. Let it flood you, body and soul. Notice how it feels warm. It reminds you of being swaddled in soft, comforting blankets as a child. You feel her around you, embracing you gently. Her love permeates you, and you feel it in your chest. You notice your heart welling up with love for her, and you can tell she is also filling you with her love for you. As you remain in her embrace, you feel at one with her. You feel a connection, one you've never had with anyone before. It's a deep connection that feels like the ground is no longer beneath your feet. Instead, you're deep in the heart of the ocean of the Dark Mother's love. Each breath makes your body thrill with joy and ecstasy. You wish you could deepen this feeling, this love you sense from her embrace. In response, you feel her presence and comfort even more intensely since she knows your desires even before you ask. You notice tears spring to your eyes, and you're fine with that. You feel you've known her for many lifetimes, and the truth is, you have.

**Conversing:** The connection is now complete. You and the Black Madonna are now bonded. She is part of your life and willing to listen to you. So, speak with her. You could speak aloud, in your mind, or under your breath. Do whatever feels natural to you. Let her know whatever is in your heart. You could ask her your questions, tell her what you desire, or just let her know you're only here to enjoy her presence and spend time with her. You could ask her for wisdom and guidance regarding a specific matter, healing, or anything else. If you don't know what to ask for, you could just keep thanking her in anticipation of the wonders she will perform in your life.

**Listening:** It's now time to sit in the silence. Sit in expectation, and the Black Virgin will respond. She may use actual words or communicate with you through feelings. She may conjure up symbols, and their meaning will become apparent to you right then or at a later time. She may simply flood your heart with her peace and love. This is how she offers guidance to you and affirms she has heard and handled your concerns.

**Becoming One with the Mother**: Now, feel your own energy. Then, shift your focus to the Black Virgin's energy. Move your attention back and forth from your energy to hers, sitting with each one for a moment. Finally, allow your energy and hers to merge. Notice how it creates something new. Notice the intuitive knowing that you're now a different person, that you have been blessed spiritually, and that blessing will play out in other aspects of your life. By merging your energies, you solidify and strengthen your bond with the Mother.

**Show Gratitude:** When you feel it's time, thank the Black Madonna for showing up for you. Thank her for guiding you and loving you unconditionally. Thank her because you know just because this meditation is coming to a close doesn't mean she will be far from you. On the contrary, she is now as close to you as you are to your beating heart. Feel her love flowing through your body and mind as you express your love and gratitude to her.

**Wrapping Up**: As slowly as possible, return your attention to your physical space by first becoming aware of your breath. Then, focus on your body and notice how you feel in it. After a few more breaths, you may open your eyes. Take a few more deep breaths, and then you're done. You have now officially accepted the Black Madonna's invitation. You now carry her presence with you, all day, every day, everywhere. You can continue strengthening the bond between you by using this guided meditation each day.

When you return to your responsibilities and plans for the day, remember you always carry her with you. Even in situations in which you can't take a moment to meditate, know you can communicate with her in your mind. You can always reach out to her at any moment you desire. What happens if you don't meditate and connect with her each day? While she'll remain with you, you may find it more difficult to notice her presence in your life. So, the onus is on you to maintain your connection to her. As for the Black Virgin, she has no intention of letting you go. You'll never have to feel alone again.

# Chapter 8: Healing through the Divine Feminine

## Divine Healing

When you experience divine healing, you know it. It's unmistakable. You feel it in your body. You notice it in the way your mind works differently. You see the way your life changes for the better. It's like a soothing balm has been spread over your heart, and all your broken bits are whole once again. Whenever you're struggling physically, spiritually, emotionally, or any other way, healing is what you need to restore you to balance.

The Divine Feminine is the force that bandages you up and makes you as good as new. It does more than heal the wounds you're conscious about. It also heals the pain you didn't realize you still have, and that's the beauty of it. Or, put more accurately, that's the beauty of the Dark Mother's healing presence in your life. You know how children always turn to their mothers whenever they're hurt, ill, or wounded? Well, you are the Black Madonna's child. You can turn to her. You're never too old or too sophisticated to take all your pain to her and ask her to show you compassion and healing. She wants you to come to her first whenever you're broken and hurt so she can fix you up and comfort you.

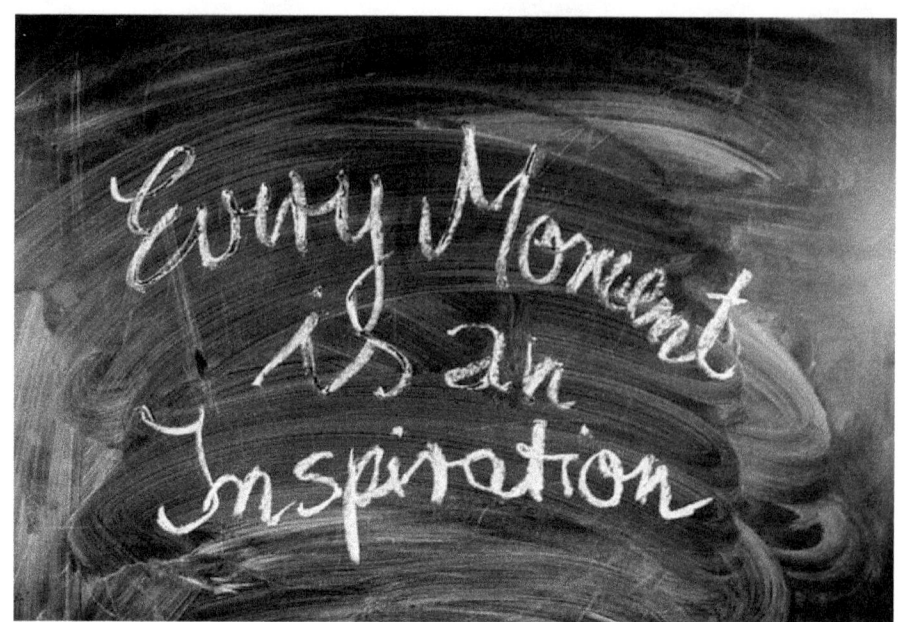

You see, choosing to allow her into your life means you will shed everything blocking your enlightenment."

What makes divine healing special is that it goes beyond dressing your emotional and spiritual wounds. The Dark Virgin does far more than fix what's broken in your life. She transforms you from the inside out. She takes your wounds and uses them to ignite the process of rebirth in your heart, giving you a new lease on life. She's not one to let you wallow in pain to get you to learn some lesson. She teaches as she heals you, making her the perfect mother. With time, you'll find she's done more than restore you to your previous state; she has helped you transcend the person you were. You'll find you've become more than the restrictive stories you used to tell and believe about yourself.

The Mother's divine healing is expressed with love, compassion, and empathy. It doesn't get any better than that. Even if you're in a place in life where you feel complete, by inviting her to be with you, you'll be surprised to find there are things that she can transform. You see, choosing to allow her into your life means you will shed everything blocking your enlightenment. Your old wounds may resurface so they can be healed fully. You'll let go of the self-doubt, pain, anger, and fear you've repressed because that was the only way to survive.

The Dark Mother is always there to help you see you're not alone. She is with you at all times. She is there to comfort you, listen to you without judgment, and help you recover from whatever has broken your spirit. She welcomes your vulnerability and accepts you as you are. Let her work her miracles in your life; you'll find every imbalance corrected. If you pay attention, you'll notice most people don't live a life of balance. They either work too much or not at all. They are in a hurry or locked to the couch. They're anxious or apathetic. If you have ever heard someone echo the sentiment, "I'm either here or there. I do extremes, no in-betweens," this is what it means to live a life without balance. Perhaps you, too, have said this once in your life or agree with the sentiment. However, that doesn't have to be the case. Remember, the Dark Virgin epitomizes balance and the integration of opposites. So, you can expect her to teach you to find peace by being balanced.

As the African Virgin heals you, you'll become a pro at aligning your energies. You'll learn how to balance your emotions. For instance, some people genuinely don't understand how to be angry with someone they love. It's as though it has to be either anger or love. They can't fathom how to balance that. So, because they want to be good partners, they'll repress their feelings whenever their partner does something that makes them angry. By the time they let their anger out, they forget this person they're skinning alive is someone they love. When harsh words have been spoken, and hurtful irreversible things have been said, they feel regret, wishing they had reined themselves in. This is just one way the Virgin teaches you how to balance your feelings and every other aspect of life. So, you see, the divine healing from the Black Madonna's love is second to none and beyond compare.

## Sophie's Healing

Sophie calls southern France her home, having lived there all her life. Ask anyone who knew her, and they would describe her as a kind, gentle, loving soul, a woman with deep, unwavering faith. Her faith was something to be admired because, for over ten years, she struggled with a debilitating condition. Each day was full of fatigue and pain. She had lived with pain for so long that she didn't remember what it felt like to not have her body aching and feeling like it was falling apart. She always believed that one day, she would find her healing. However, she didn't know how. Her medication only did so much, and some days, she almost lost her faith. Still, she persevered.

One day, a friend swung by Sophie's place with several books for her as she loved to read. Once alone, she picked up the stack of books to see which one she'd get into first. However, the one on the Black Madonna fell on the floor. It fell awkwardly, open and face down on the ground. Carefully, she reached down to pick it up. Her gut said to read the page that it had fallen open on. So, she did. It turned out that page was about how the Black Madonna heals anyone who asks for her help. At that moment, it felt as though a light went on in her heart. She knew in her heart she had been waiting for this moment.

Sophie would excitedly ring her friend the next day and ask to be taken to the closest Black Madonna shrine. It wasn't an easy journey for Sophie since her body was battered and hurting. Still, with a smile on her lips and a heart full of hope and positive expectation, she made it. When she got to the shrine, she gasped at the statue of the Black Madonna. It was breathtaking to her. It seemed to beckon her closer, and it moved her so deeply she moved closer to it, tears streaming down her face and prayer springing from her lips. She allowed herself to share her pain with the Black Virgin. She cried, "I've had to carry this pain for far too long. Please. I know you are the one I have been waiting for. I know I was meant to be here now. I know you can help me, Black Madonna. I offer you my body, and I ask you to heal me." She reached out to touch the Black Madonna, and while her body still hurt, she felt profound peace in that instant. It was undeniable. Sophie knew the Black Madonna was real and present.

As the days and weeks passed, Sophie experienced a change in her body. She became more flexible. The aches and pains were fewer and fewer. Even her skin would grow rosier and younger looking. She did nothing different. She didn't take new medication, nor did she change her diet. Each day, she grew stronger. At her next medical checkup, her doctor was so astounded she called the other doctors to witness Sophie's miraculous recovery. They scratched their heads, theorized, and analyzed but could not find a scientifically sound reason for Sophie's healing. Sophie told them, "That's because the Black Madonna is beyond science!" Of course, most of them thought she was kooky, but Sophie didn't care. She was healed. She now makes it her duty to visit the Black Madonna's shrine regularly and share her story with anyone within earshot.

# Fatima's Healing

Fatima had a loving relationship with her family. They had a lovely connection with one another, sharing their hopes and dreams, encouraging one another, and enjoying the love they had. Her childhood home was a safe haven, and there was never a moment when she would feel unloved or unheard. However, that would be ruined when a friend she'd invited to her home would tell her a malicious lie. It was a cruel lie. This "friend" of Fatima's had accused her brother, Ahmed, of abusing her. The lie was so vile it rocked the family to its core. The accusation was a grave one, so, of course, Fatima confronted her brother. The story was so horrific, and her friend was a master deceiver, so it was tough to believe Ahmed was innocent. The confrontation would become so intense that it utterly destroyed Fatima's connection with her loved ones. She believed her narcissistic friend so much that she felt duty-bound to stand by this person. Fatima's family was so angry and frustrated with her that they would eventually decide to oust her.

Fatima was shocked at being rejected by the people she called family. Not one person even bothered to call her after to learn how she was doing or where she had gone. She was angry. She was hurt. She was lonely. She thought she could count on her friend but would eventually discover one of this person's other lies. She had to cut ties with them at that point, so she felt truly alone. Weeks became months, months because years, and Fatima had grown used to being alone. She became distrustful and taught herself to live alone. She convinced herself she didn't need anyone and suppressed her loneliness. It was only a matter of time before Fatima's depression grew too much to bear.

One evening, tired of hiding in the small room of the tiny apartment she'd scrounged some money to rent, she decided to take a walk. The depressing and suicidal thoughts were becoming too much to bear, and she had learned taking walks was a good way to handle them. This evening, she felt compelled to take a different route than she was used to. So, she followed the urge. As she walked, she noticed a Black Madonna image beside a doorway. Curious, she stopped and stared at it, mesmerized. An old man opened the door and smiled at Fatima. "She wants to see you if you want to see her." He beckoned her in and walked ahead, not waiting to see if she followed him into the Black Madonna sanctuary. Fatima had a brief moment when she wanted to keep walking, but she thought to herself, "Well, if he's going to take my life, at least he'll put me out of my misery." She used to be such a bright, happy person, but now, thoughts like this had become the norm for her.

Fatima entered, and inside, she saw a statue of the Black Madonna. It was life-sized, but she felt it was larger than life. She was immediately drawn to the statue. As if in a trance, she walked toward the statue and began hitting it, screaming and crying. While she did that, it was as if no one else was in the room with her. It was only her and the Black Madonna. No one stopped her. She kept going, and eventually, she stopped hitting the statue and hugged it, and her screams died down to whimpers. "Please fix me. Please fix us." She repeated this simple prayer over and over. Eventually, she would fall asleep at the feet of the Black Virgin. Her hosts were warm and kind, and they took care of her until she left the next day. She felt lighter in her heart, and there was a pep in her step. The Black Mother had healed her. She showed Fatima that her family may have rejected her, but she had always been there. The Black Mother was her mother, father, brother, and sister. She was her friend and confidante.

Fatima practiced connecting with the Black Madonna daily, faithfully basking in her presence and receiving deep insights. She had wanted to reach out to her family, but the Mother told her there was no need. Six months after the evening at the Black Madonna sanctuary, her phone would ring. It was an unfamiliar number, and usually, Fatima made a point of avoiding calls from numbers she didn't recognize. As her phone rang this time, it felt like time froze still. It felt like a date with destiny to her, and it was. When she answered, the voice on the other end belonged to her father. They arranged to meet with the rest of the family. Needless to say, the reunion was intense and healing for all. Fatima got the chance to apologize to Ahmed, and her family apologized for abandoning her. In doing this, their emotional wounds were healed. The Black Mother fueled the forgiveness and understanding among them with her essence. Fatima's faith in the Mother is now stronger than ever.

Sophie's and Fatima's stories are only two of thousands upon thousands that demonstrate the divine healing power of the Black Madonna. There is no wound too deep for her to heal and no rift she cannot fix.

# The Dark Mother's Nurturing Qualities

Would you like to know how the Dark Mother can care for you? Here's a close look at the Black Madonna's traits, specifically regarding her role as a nurturer, which is an expression of the Divine feminine.

**She Offers Unconditional Love.** The moment you decide to connect with the Divine Feminine, you'll find her love embracing you. The Dark Mother is as tender as she is powerful. She doesn't need you to be or do anything special before she shows you her love. Look at Fatima, for instance. She made an honest mistake, but the African Mother didn't care. She didn't get angry at Fatima's way of expressing her pain and grief. She loved and still loves her, regardless. The Mother feels the same about you.

**She Is Always Compassionate and Full of Empathy.** She gets you. This isn't just some sentence to make you feel warm and fuzzy. The Dark Mother really does understand and empathize with you. More than anyone else, she knows the sorrows you experience. She feels your joy and your pain. So, whenever you feel challenged or feel as if life is too much, remember she's right with you. She's there to shoulder your burdens. If you need someone to listen without judgment, turn to her; she will offer you her ears and heart.

**She Protects and Comforts You.** In the middle of a storm, you can trust her with your worries and fears. You will feel your fears melt away as you realize the Divine Feminine within you is greater than anything that could come against you. You can take comfort in her loving embrace and allow that to fuel your heart with courage.

**She Heals You and Renews Your Life**. Whether you're dealing with a scraped knee or a battered heart, she will bring you healing. She is ease, flow, and rejuvenation. Her presence in your life keeps things fresh, making it impossible for any wound to fester and take you down.

**She Gives You Strength.** When you have a challenge or a struggle, you can count on her to fuel you with the fortitude you need to persevere. Just when you think you're all tapped out, she emerges as your second wind, helping you deal with your issues with uncommon grace.

# Healing through Devotion

You can use prayer, healing rituals, sacred healing dance, and similar techniques to help you connect to the healing power of the Black Madonna.

## The Power of Prayer

By praying, you can connect with the Black Madonna. Praying doesn't require special clothes or circumstances. It is inner work because you only need an open heart with clear intentions. Praying involves having a conversation with the Divine Feminine. You can share your feelings and thoughts with her or simply state your intentions and ask her to bless them. You can request healing, and she will answer you.

**How:** Before you start your day, take five to ten minutes to sit in silence and shut your eyes. After a few deep breaths, you may begin to speak with the Black Madonna. Tell her what you would like her to heal. Share your dreams and fears. She is a confidante, so you can tell her everything and anything. When you're done, sit in silence and wait for any insights. You may also sit in silence until you feel peace, which confirms you've been heard and your prayer is answered.

## Healing Rituals

A ritual is a ceremony with a precise sequence of events and certain elements that make it special. Rituals can be elaborate or simple. You may light a candle, burn some incense, set up an altar and pray at it, or do all these and more. The idea is rituals cause the energy of the Black Madonna to come through stronger because you're being intentional in your desire to connect with her as you perform the ritual. The ritual can demonstrate your love for the Mother, and on top of that, it's a channel that allows her healing love to flow through you and to you.

**How:** Designate a small area of your home as a sacred space. If you have some sage, you can burn it to cleanse the energy of this space first. Get a picture or carving of the Black Madonna and place it in this space, on the floor, or on a table, which will become your dedicated altar. If you have any other items that remind you of the Black Madonna, you can set them with the statue or artwork, too. When preparing to perform a ritual, you should always start by cleansing the space with sage. Then, light a candle, sit with your eyes shut for a few moments, and take some deep breaths to center yourself. When you're relaxed and still, you can open your eyes and contemplate the Black Madonna. Or, keep your eyes shut and pray or meditate on her essence. When you have finished, always allow the candle to go out by itself, and thank her for honoring you with her presence. Please never leave a burning candle or incense unattended.

### Sacred Healing Dance

Your body is intelligent. One of the ways it can express that intelligence is through dance. As you dance, you express yourself. Dancing with the intention of experiencing the Black Madonna's healing in your life will definitely draw that power to you. By engaging in sacred healing dances, you release the emotions that are pent up within you. You accept her solace and comfort, healing, guidance, and more.

**How:** Pick any music reminiscent of the essence of the Black Mother. It should uplift you spiritually, and it's best if it has no lyrics to distract you. Find somewhere private and peaceful in your home or a peaceful area outdoors. Allow your body to move. Think of the music as a question and your body's movements as the answer. You can turn your brain off by feeling your body as you move. Notice how different movements affect you. Allow your emotions to come out through your body however they want. This isn't for Broadway: this is to allow the Divine Mother's energy to flow through you so you can heal, so keep this intention front and center in your mind.

# Chapter 9: Honoring the Mother Goddess

People honor the Black Madonna in various ways, whether alone or as a community. By understanding how people show their devotion to the Virgin, you, too, will know how you can show her your life and appreciation.

## Altars and Shrines

All over the world, you can find shrines in the Black Madonna's honor. Public shrines are large enough to cater to many devotees at once. How do you set up your own altar? People set up altars in their homes to honor the Mother even when they're nowhere near a shrine. Well, first, you need to have a sacred space. As you set up your altar, you need to be intentional about it. Pick a space that feels right or somewhere meaningful to you and the others around you who are devoted to the Black Madonna. This is no ordinary space. It's a portal that will allow the Mother's energy to come through powerfully.

One main element of an altar or shrine is art. You need depictions of the Black Madonna, whether paintings, sculptures, or both. They are more than representations of the Divine Feminine; they are also portals allowing the Divine and the earthly to merge. Placing them in your shrine or on your altar gives everyone something to focus on as they pray, meditate, or contemplate.

You're also going to need candles. Now that you have the Virgin's presence in your heart, the candle's flame represents the inner divine light that shines within you. As you light a candle, you perform a ritual. You draw on the warm and loving energies of the Mother and make it easier for inner alchemy to occur within you as you remain at the altar or shrine. Since the Mother has a connection with nature, you may want to include flowers and foliage on the altar to honor this aspect of the Madonna. When you use fresh flowers, they represent the ideas of growth and inner beauty. As for greenery, that represents the fertility of the Divine Mother and her ability to renew you and bless you abundantly.

If you wish, you can add other items that mean something to you or your community and connect you to the Black Virgin. You may feel inspired to add seashells, special stones and crystals, water vessels, and even drawn or carved symbols to draw even more of her energy to the altar or shine. When you have set up your altar, you can make offerings to her. Your offering could be as simple as a glass of water. It could take more work, like a well-prepared meal. You could offer other items that are dear to you. It doesn't matter what you offer as long as you're intuitively led to offer that item, and you do so with a true sense of appreciation for the Black Mother. When you're not busy appreciating her at the altar or shrine, you may simply contemplate her essence or reflect on the insights she has given you.

## Candlelight Vigils

It's the light of the soul and the light of the Divine Feminine who nurtures you and keeps you safe and warm.⁴⁶

Devotees of the Black Virgin also have candlelight vigils in her honor. These are no ordinary rituals. They are meant to revere her and to unite everyone in her love. Each flame represents the inner light of divinity each devotee has within them. It's the light of the soul and the light of the Divine Feminine who nurtures you and keeps you safe and warm. Candlelight vigils are excellent for unifying communities. The energy of warmth and solidarity is palpable. Everyone stands together, staring intently into the candle flame in their hand. If you ever get the chance to be part of a vigil, you should go. You'll be glad you attended.

## Festivals and Pilgrimages

People honor and celebrate the Black Virgin through festivals and by making pilgrimages. Pilgrimages are trips to sacred sites and often have people from all over the world participating. The festivals are full of joy and light; everyone is fully aware of their spiritual nature and connection to others and the Divine. You can find these festivals wherever shrines or sites are dedicated to the Black Virgin. For instance, there is the Madonna of Altötting. Each year, at least one million faithful make their way to Altötting to thank her and pray for her miracles and blessings at Our Lady Altötting, which is in the Chapel of Mercy or Gnadenkapelle (Chapel of Mercy). You may also enjoy the Sara Gypsy Festival, which is held in the Camargue. Expect to meet gypsies by the thousands at this festival as they come to honor the Black Madonna.

Festivals and pilgrimages are excellent for cultural expression and communing with like-minded people. You experience a spiritual connection unlike anything else when you partake in them. There are ceremonies and rituals, prayers, processions, and more. Also, there are always miracles and testimonies. The spiritual importance of the Black Virgin's sites and shrines cannot be overstated. They offer physical points of contact for those who know the Mother and those who don't to experience her powerfully. Typically, the sites are serene places with interesting histories and incorporate elements of nature. When you take a trip to these places, you can consider your journey a metaphor for your inner alchemical journey. The following is a list of annual holy days and feast days in honor of the Black Madonna and their locations. Remember that the dates may vary depending on what's going on in the location, and there may be alterations to the liturgical calendars. Also, this is not an exhaustive list.

1. **Feast of Our Lady of Częstochowa:** August 26th, at the Jasna Góra Monastery, Częstochowa, Poland.
2. **Feast of Our Lady of Lourdes:** February 11th, at the Sanctuary of Our Lady of Lourdes, Lourdes, France.
3. **Feast of Our Lady of Montserrat:** April 27th, at the Montserrat Monastery, Catalonia, Spain.
4. **Feast of Our Lady of Prompt Succor:** January 8th, at the National Shrine of Our Lady of Prompt Succor, New Orleans, Louisiana, United States of America.
5. **Feast of Our Lady of Guadalupe:** December 12th, at the Basilica of Our Lady of Guadalupe, Mexico City, Mexico.
6. **Feast of Our Lady of Regla:** September 8th, at the Basilica of Nuestra Señora de Regla, Regla, Cuba.
7. **Feast of Our Lady of Montevergine**: February 2nd, at the Abbey of Montevergine, Naples, Southern Italy. (This event is dear to the LGBT community, as the Madonna of Montevergine has historically been of help to them, going as far back as medieval times.)
8. **Feast of Our Lady of Einsiedeln:** September 14th, at the Einsiedeln Abbey, Einsiedeln, Switzerland.
9. **Feast of our Lady of Candelaria:** February 2nd, at the Basilica of Candelaria, Tenerife, Canary Islands, Spain.
10. **Feast of Our Lady of Altötting:** September $12^{th}$, at the Chapel of Grace, Altötting, Germany.
11. **Feast of Our Lady of Tindari**: September 8th, at the Sanctuary of Tindari, Sicily, Italy.
12. **Feast of Our Lady of Walsingham:** September 24th, at the Shrine of Our Lady of Walsingham, Norfolk, England.
13. **Feast of Our Lady of Africa:** April 20th, at the Notre Dame d'Afrique, Algiers, Algeria.
14. **Feast of Mary, Divine Mother (Solemnity of Mary, Mother of God):** January 1st, at Catholic Churches worldwide.

## Meditation and Contemplation

Black Madonna devotees recognize the importance of the twin practices of meditation and contemplation because they make it easier to connect with the energy of the Divine Feminine and keep it flowing in their lives. They realize that the Black Madonna's guidance becomes clearer when they spend time doing these things. Meditation is about keeping your attention on one thing, whether an object, your breath, or a mantra or affirmation, to help you become more mindful of the moment and in general.

On the other hand, contemplation involves bringing a specific interest or concern to mind, sitting with it mindfully, exploring every aspect of it that you can, and coming up with profound insights on the subject. You may contemplate the Black Madonna, an aspect of her being, a symbol, or anything else you desire.

You already know how to meditate. Now, the question is, how do you contemplate? Specifically, how do you contemplate the Black Madonna to honor her?

*A good way to adjust the ambiance of the space would be to use one or more candles rather than daylight or even harsher electrical light.*⁴⁷

**Location:** Pick a quiet and comfy spot, distraction-free and welcoming. You should enjoy being in this place. A good way to adjust the ambiance of the space would be to use one or more candles rather than daylight or even harsher electrical light. When you light incense, you make the atmosphere feel even more sacred. This is excellent for your contemplation.

**Intention:** Choose which aspect of the Madonna you would like to contemplate. Do you want to mine gold from the idea of integrating opposites? Would you like to make peace with darkness and see what gifts it has to offer you? Do you want to understand how to allow more of the Black Madonna's alchemical transformation or spiritual healing? Figure out your intention.

Whatever you have chosen, craft a short question that summarizes what you'd like to contemplate. For instance, you could ask, "How can I allow more ease in my life with the Black Madonna's help?" This will be your anchor question. You'll understand why you need it soon. If you like, you can also contemplate something physical, like her statue, picture, or anything you have that resonates with you and instantly reminds you of the Black Mother. If you wish, you may contemplate her eyes, skin, outstretched arms, or any element in her visual depiction to which you are drawn.

**Contemplation:** Contemplate whatever you've settled on. Shut your eyes, take a few deep breaths to anchor you to the here and now, and help you feel still and centered. When you notice the distinct peace that comes when you meditate, you may open your eyes and look at whatever you want to contemplate. If it's not visual, keep your eyes closed and allow your mind to explore your chosen subject.

Contemplation isn't something you force. You cannot rush the process, either. Take your time with this. If you can, do it at a time when you don't have any obligations so you're not subconsciously rushing yourself. Allow the thoughts and inner impressions to rise on their own within you. If you find you're wandering from your contemplation onto other thoughts, use your anchor question to bring you back. You may ask the question aloud, softly, or in your mind. This question will anchor you to the purpose of your contemplation.

You might have a new question as your mind lights up with insights. You can write that down to be the subject matter of your next contemplation if you need more time with the present matter. However, if you feel satisfied with what you have received so far and you still have time, you may contemplate the next thing. Note that it would be best to have a journal to make notes. If you find writing slow and tedious, use a recording app to speak your thoughts aloud and later transcribe them. It's always handy to have them in written form so you can read through them whenever you want or skip to particularly profound points from your contemplation that you'd like to ponder.

**Integration:** Now that you have received insight, it's time to make it useful. Why does that matter? You're not contemplating spiritual matters simply for the sake of knowledge. It's one thing to not know something and not act on it. After all, how can you act on information you don't have? It's another thing to have knowledge and do nothing with it or about it. Ground the wisdom you receive in practicality. Write or state at least three ways you can make it practical in your life. If it helps, consider each part of your life and come up with three things you'll do differently in each one, whether that's in your personal relationships, professional life, health, spiritual walk, and so on.

**Conclusion:** When you're done contemplating, you'll know it. It feels like being complete, for lack of a better way to describe it. When you arrive at this feeling, shut your eyes once more and thank the Black Madonna for her wisdom and guidance. Thank her in advance for helping you integrate the insights you've received from the contemplation into your daily life. You see, you have your inner will and determination, but those things can only get you so far. You'll have phenomenal results by asking and thanking her for the grace and strength to follow through on implementing what you've learned.

When you can't find it in you to do the right, wise thing, the Dark Virgin will step in and fuel you with the strength you need. You are expressing complete trust in her by thanking her right after your contemplation for helping with this. You're telling her you know she will help you with your mission of inner transformation. That sort of faith pleases her, and she'll be more than happy to prove you were right to trust her even before you had evidence of her help and blessing in your life.

## Why Devotion Matters

You need to devote yourself to the Black Madonna to maintain your relationship with her. As you express this devotion, you'll be transformed in many ways and always for the better. By being deliberate about reaching out to her, you show her your love and nurture your bond with her. You also make it impossible for her blessings and healing not to flow to you. When you are devoted to the Divine Feminine, your spiritual life is set on fire, burning brighter, revealing more of your true self. You go beyond mere dogma and doctrine, as you have actual experiences of the divine. This is the benefit that devotion offers you.

Devotion is a way to allow yourself to heal on the inside, too. By deliberately bringing yourself to the Black Madonna's presence daily, you give her room to work on your wounds. She'll fix your traumas. She'll go through the past and mend what's broken in you. There's no better space to let her help with your emotional wounds than during devotion. Devotion is a service you offer the Black Madonna from your heart, from a place of truth and reverence. Some people think of her only when they need something, but they only shortchange themselves by doing this. With devotion, you come to her and relate with her as you would a friend. No one likes that one friend who only calls them when they need something. The Black Madonna is obviously not one to be phased by that, but it's only fair and right for you to make devotion a daily practice. As you do so, you'll experience more miracles and blessings. You'll gain more wisdom, and your spiritual development will soar.

By devoting yourself to the Dark Virgin, you build a bridge that takes you from mere head knowledge to heart knowledge of all spiritual matters. You're different from those who are talented at sounding like they know what they're talking about but don't have actual experiences with the Mother. You live her. You breathe her. She is as real to you as the words on this page. All that happens when you decide to devote yourself to her is to set up daily practices to remind yourself of her presence and benevolence in your life.

Devotion makes the ineffable tangible in your life. You will know, without a doubt, that there is more to life than your physical senses can pick up on. Devotion is like taking a daily drink from the eternally flowing river of life that is the Black Mother. It brings you peace. It helps you see beyond the illusions of the physical world, as it makes it easier for the Madonna to demonstrate her presence and remind you there's no one greater than her. So, when challenges, obstacles, and adversity rear their heads and seem insurmountable, you relax. You know, through devotion, you have a presence within you that is greater than anything the world could throw at you.

# Conclusion

You now believe she is calling you, don't you? This book may have come to an end, but there is unfinished business between you and the Black Madonna. Something hangs in the air, waiting for you to dictate what happens next. Her invitation remains extended, her outstretched hands waiting, desiring you to reach out and take them with yours so she can show you the path to fulfillment, growth, freedom, and joy. You now know what her offer entails. You know what to expect from her and understand what is expected of you. Will you set this book down when you're done and continue about your business as if you can't see her asking you to let her make your life beautiful? Or will you take the leap, trusting that she will heal you on every level? Will you let her transform your life for the better? Will you accept her offer of peace and ease? Will you let her teach you what she knows so you can use the wisdom she offers to craft a life that aligns with your true self? You alone can answer that.

Through this book, you've been introduced to the enigma that is the Black Mother. You know how to recognize her presence. You feel a strong resonance with her, and this is no accident. You've discovered this benevolent force that can offer you spiritual transformation and show you the wonders and mysteries of the eternal Divine Feminine. You've learned how she blesses one and all and never discriminates in offering guidance, protection, and profound wisdom to those who seek her out and call upon her. You may have come to the conclusion of this book, but when it comes to your story with her, it remains incomplete. If you'd like to know how it goes, you have to trust her. Why not? There are so many reasons to accept her in your life.

The Dark Mother is resilience itself. She is a testament that you can endure the worst of the worst and still come out on top, transformed into the best version of yourself yet. That's the beauty of having a relationship with her. There's no cap on how much better things can get for you. She's in the business of leaving your jaw hanging with awe and gratitude as she takes you from height to height while you continue to honor her steadfastly in devotion. She's seen it all, from the rise and fall of kingdoms and empires to trials and triumphs that humanity has faced collectively and individually. She knows how ugly humanity can get, yet she is equally aware of your potential to thrive and soar. Your Divine Mother wants you to know your potential and to make it real.

If you say yes to her, be warned that you will never remain the same. Your transformation will be so brilliant and beautiful that you'll hardly be able to recognize the person you were before you read this book. The Black Madonna will show you she is not some far-off god who picks and chooses who gets their prayers answered. She will be a loving friend, mother, and guide, right by your side, steering you down the paths you should take. You may feel some regret about not having known her before now or wasting time waffling between whether or not you should surrender your life to her. However, don't waste your time this way. You are exactly where you should be. Moreover, you can rest knowing she doesn't care for calendars or clocks. The Black Madonna is never late.

# Appendix: List of Black Madonnas

Our Lady of Consolation of the Dejected and Oppressed

Our Lady of Consolation of the Dejected and Oppressed.⁴⁶

## Our Lady of Deliverance

Our Lady of Deliverance.⁴⁹

Virgin Mary of Einsiedeln

Virgin Mary of Einsiedeln.[50]

## Our Lady of Guadalupe

Our Lady of Guadalupe.[51]

# The Virgin of Juquila

The Virgin of Juquila.⁶⁸

# Our Lady of Loreto

Our Lady of Loreto.[58]

## Our Lady of Altötting

**Our Lady of Altötting.**[54]

# Notre Dame de la Sarte

Notre Dame de la Sarte.[55]

# La Vierge Noire d'Outremeuse

**La Vierge Noire d'Outremeuse.**[56]

# The Black Virgin

The Black Virgin.[87]

Marija Bistrica

Marija Bistrica.[58]

## Nuestra Señora de la Caridad del Cobre

Nuestra Señora de la Caridad del Cobre.[59]

# The Eleousa of Kykkos

The Eleousa of Kykkos.[60]

If you enjoyed this book, I'd greatly appreciate a review on Amazon because it helps me to create more books that people want. It would mean a lot to hear from you.

**To leave a review:**
1. Open your camera app.
2. Point your mobile device at the QR code.
3. The review page will appear in your web browser.

---

*Thanks for your support!*

# Here's another book by Mari Silva that you might like

# Your Free Gift
# (only available for a limited time)

Thanks for getting this book! If you want to learn more about various spirituality topics, then join Mari Silva's community and get a free guided meditation MP3 for awakening your third eye. This guided meditation mp3 is designed to open and strengthen ones third eye so you can experience a higher state of consciousness. Simply visit the link below the image to get started.

https://spiritualityspot.com/meditation

## Or, Scan the QR code!

# References

(N.d.). Greekmythology.com. https://www.greekmythology.com/Other_Gods/Persephone/persephone.html

(N.d.). Greekmythology.com. https://www.greekmythology.com/Myths/Norse/Skadi/skadi.html

(N.d.). Owlcation.com. https://owlcation.com/humanities/TheCailleach

10 Benefits to Building Altars in Your Home. (n.d.). AuthorsDen.Com. https://www.authorsden.com/visit/viewarticle.asp?id=21959&AuthorID=32186

8 Phases Of The Moon — The Hoodwitch. (n.d.). The Hoodwitch. https://www.thehoodwitch.com/8-phases-of-the-moon

Abiola. (2016, May 14). Ala, Igbo goddess of Fertility and imagination! Today's African goddess affirmation card. Womanifest Your Power with Abiola: Spirit, Mindset, Success. https://womanifesting.com/ala-igbo-goddess-creativity/

Aesthetic, H. (2022, January 6). Goddess Chinnamastā or Pracaṇḍacaṇḍikā - hindu aesthetic - Medium. Medium. https://hinduaesthetic.medium.com/goddess-chinnamast%C4%81-c2786af73204

Africa, A. (2021, April 27). The Ancient Beliefs of African Goddesses. Amplify Africa. https://www.amplifyafrica.org/the-ancient-beliefs-of-african-goddesses/

Ala - Myth Encyclopedia - mythology, god, snake, life, people, African. (n.d.). Mythencyclopedia.com. http://www.mythencyclopedia.com/A-Am/Ala.html

Aletheia. (2015, April 4). What is shadow work? 7 exercises (+ free workbook). LonerWolf. https://lonerwolf.com/shadow-work-demons/

Amorim, K. (2019a, February 10). Durga - the warrior motherly goddess. -. Komala Amorim. https://www.komalaamorim.com/durga-the-warrior-motherly-goddess/

Amorim, K. (2019b, February 10). Kali - goddess of transformation, destruction, and transcendent energy -. Komala Amorim. https://www.komalaamorim.com/kali-goddess-of-transformation-destruction-and-transcendent-energy/

Andrews, A. M. (n.d.). The Divine Colors of Hathor. http://www.jewelry-history.com/2014/07/the-divine-colors-of-hathor.html

Angrboda (Giantess). (n.d.). Vikings Wiki; Fandom, Inc. https://vikings.fandom.com/wiki/Angrboda_(Giantess)

Bell, J. G. (2023, July 1). Nyx Goddess of the Night. The Hermetic Library Blog. https://library.hrmtc.com/2023/07/01/nyx-goddess-of-the-night/

Birch, L. (2022, March 3). Morana's Frozen Howl — A Deity for Angry Non-Binary Witches. Medium. https://lunarbirch.medium.com/moranas-frozen-howl-a-deity-for-angry-non-binary-witches-3dd05265b5a3

Cailleach - Mythopedia. (n.d.). Mythopedia. https://mythopedia.com/topics/cailleach

Cartwright, M. (2013). Kali. World History Encyclopedia. https://www.worldhistory.org/Kali/

Cartwright, M. (2021). The Mórrigan. World History Encyclopedia. https://www.worldhistory.org/The_Morrigan/

Chamunda Maa: The Hindu goddess of safety and protection. (2023a, February 22). Pujasthan. https://www.pujasthan.com/chamunda-maa-story-mantra-history/

Chiat, J. (n.d.). Russia Maslenitsa Festival - All You Can Eat Pancakes - Expat Explore. https://expatexplore.com/blog/maslenitsa-festival-russia-pancake-week/

Chinnamasta - the goddess who cut her head -. (2021, December 26). Hinduism Facts; Rahul. https://www.hinduismfacts.org/hindu-gods-and-goddesses/chinnamasta/

Complete chinnamasta mahavidya. (n.d.). Siddhaguru.org. https://www.siddhaguru.org/en/sri-chinnamasta-mahavidya

Cuba, A. pa mi. (2021a, April 26). What powers does the Orisha Yewá represent in the Yoruba Religion? Ashé pa mi Cuba. https://ashepamicuba.com/en/yewa-yoruba/

Cuba, A. pa mi. (2021b, September 1). Did you know these interesting qualities of Yewá? Goddess guess and pure. Ashé pa mi Cuba. https://ashepamicuba.com/en/orisha-yewa/

DanFF. (2022, March 17). Goddess Nyx - Greek Primordial Goddess of the Night. Santuário Lunar (Moon Shrine). https://www.santuariolunar.com/goddess-nyx/?expand_article=1

Dark Goddesses in Today's Society. (n.d.). The Veiled Crow. https://www.veiledcrow.com/service-page/dark-goddesses-in-today-s-society

Das, S. (2007, June 15). 10 of the most important Hindu gods. Learn Religions. https://www.learnreligions.com/top-hindu-deities-1770309

Das, S. (2008, April 16). Kali: The Dark Mother goddess in Hinduism. Learn Religions. https://www.learnreligions.com/kali-the-dark-mother-1770364

Davidson, L. (n.d.). Sekhmet: The ancient Egyptian goddess of war. History Hit. https://www.historyhit.com/sekhmet-the-ancient-egyptian-goddess-of-war/

Deleted. (n.d.). Hecate in different mythologies : r/mythology. https://www.reddit.com/r/mythology/comments/nipys7/hecate_in_different_mythologies/

DK Find Out! (n.d.). DK Find Out! https://www.dkfindout.com/us/history/ancient-egypt/sekhmet/

Domitrovich, M. (2015, September 27). The invocation of Kali. EDIBLESPIRIT. https://ediblespirit.com/eatyourspirit/2015/9/27/trim-your-dingleberries-or-the-invocation-of-kali

Dunlop, S. (n.d.-a). Macha. Bardmythologies.com. https://bardmythologies.com/macha/

Dunlop, S. (n.d.-b). The curse of Macha. Bardmythologies.com. https://bardmythologies.com/the-curse-of-macha/

Ebede, F. (2023, March 3). Dark Feminine Energy: How To Embrace It And Unleash Your Inner Goddess. Selfhealjourney.Com. https://selfhealjourney.com/2023/03/03/dark-feminine-energy/

Eclectic Witchcraft. (2023, October 13). Ways To Represent Lilith On Your Pagan Altar - Eclectic Witchcraft. https://eclecticwitchcraft.com/ways-to-represent-lilith-on-your-pagan-altar/

Ereškigal (goddess). (n.d.). http://oracc.museum.upenn.edu/amgg/listofdeities/erekigal/index.html

Establishing the temple of Nephthys. (2021, December 19). Isiopolis. https://isiopolis.com/2021/12/19/establishing-the-temple-of-nephthys/

Eze, C. (2023, March 19). Oya, the Yoruba rain goddess. The Guardian Nigeria News - Nigeria and World News; Guardian Nigeria. https://guardian.ng/life/oya-the-yoruba-rain-goddess/

Fields, K. (2018, December 20). Dark Goddesses: Our 15 FAVORITES From Around the World. Otherworldly Oracle. https://otherworldlyoracle.com/dark-goddesses-list-descriptions/

Fields, K. (2019, November 25). Hathor Goddess of Love: How to work with her for Love & passion. Otherworldly Oracle; FIELDS CREATIVE CONSULTING. https://otherworldlyoracle.com/egyptian-goddess-of-love/

Goddess Ala. (2012, March 14). Journeying to the Goddess. https://journeyingtothegoddess.wordpress.com/2012/03/14/goddess-ala/

Goddess Baba Yaga. (2013, June 7). Journeying to the Goddess. https://journeyingtothegoddess.wordpress.com/2012/08/31/goddess-baba-yaga/

Goddess Hathor: Three ways of mentoring the dead. -. (2020, May 18). María Rosa Valdesogo. https://www.mariarosavaldesogo.com/goddess-hathor-three-ways-mentoring-the-dead/

Goddess Hecate Moon Phase Necklace, Triple Goddess Symbol — Bang-Up Betty. (n.d.). Bang-Up Betty. https://www.bangupbetty.com/siren/hecate-moon-phase-necklace

Goddess Kali. (2013, June 7). Journeying to the Goddess. https://journeyingtothegoddess.wordpress.com/2012/02/24/goddess-kali/

Hair, Hathor and moon. (2013, July 7). HAIR AND DEATH IN ANCIENT EGYPT. https://hairanddeathinancientegypt.com/2013/07/08/hathor-moon-and-hair/

Hannah. (2022, February 14). Comparing Egyptian, Roman, and Greek gods - Hannah Fielding. Hannah Fielding. https://hannahfielding.net/egyptian-roman-greek-gods/

Hardy, J. (2023, April 24). Chaos and Destruction: The symbolism of Angrboda in Norse Mythology and Beyond | History Cooperative. History Cooperative. https://historycooperative.org/angrboda/

Hardy, J. (2023a, March 10). Skadi: The Norse goddess of skiing, hunting, and pranks. History Cooperative; The History Cooperative. https://historycooperative.org/skadi/

Hathor. (n.d.). Mythopedia. https://mythopedia.com/topics/hathor

Heal the Soul through Meditation. (2019, April 21). Science of Spirituality. https://www.sos.org/heal-the-soul-through-meditation/

Hel (The Underworld). (2012, November 15). Norse Mythology for Smart People. https://norse-mythology.org/cosmology/the-nine-worlds/helheim/

Hel. (n.d.). Mythos and Legends Wiki; Fandom, Inc. https://mythos-and-legends.fandom.com/wiki/Hel

Herukhuti, R. A. (2023, October 14). Nut: The Black Mother Goddess of Egypt. Afrikaiswoke.com. https://www.afrikaiswoke.com/nut-the-black-mother-goddess-of-egypt/

Hirst, K. K. (2019, October 28). Marzanna, Slavic Goddess of Death and Winter. ThoughtCo. https://www.thoughtco.com/marzanna-4774267

Hoseck, N. (2023, January 31). The Morrigan: A goddess of fate, war, and death. Ireland Wide. https://www.irelandwide.com/the-morrigan/

How to embrace & integrate your shadow self for major healing. (2021, November 11). Mindbodygreen. https://www.mindbodygreen.com/articles/shadow-self

Huanaco, F. (2022, February 11). Persephone: Goddess Correspondences, Symbols & Myth. Spells8. https://spells8.com/lessons/persephone-goddess/

Inana/Ištar (goddess). (n.d.). http://oracc.museum.upenn.edu/amgg/listofdeities/inanaitar/

Insight Network, Inc. (n.d.). Awaken The Dark Moon Goddess Within. Insighttimer.Com. https://insighttimer.com/soulvisionary/guided-meditations/awaken-the-dark-moon-goddess-within

Iwalaiye, T. (2023, March 3). African deities: Who is goddess Oya? Pulse Nigeria. https://www.pulse.ng/lifestyle/food-travel/african-deities-who-is-goddess-oya/q5gf7h2

Jay, S. (2022, July 18). How To Embrace Dark Feminine Energy & Unleash Your Power. Revoloon. https://revoloon.com/shanijay/dark-feminine-energy

Jessica, S. (2019, July 28). Angrboda Norse mythology. Norse and Viking Mythology; vkngjewelry. https://blog.vkngjewelry.com/en/angrboda/

Joe, J. (2022a, January 11). Nephthys: The ancient Egyptian goddess of air and betrayal. Timeless Myths. https://www.timelessmyths.com/mythology/nephthys/

Joe, J. (2022b, March 8). Sekhmet: The warrior goddess and protector of the Egyptian pharaohs. Timeless Myths. https://www.timelessmyths.com/mythology/sekhmet/

JSouthernStudio. (n.d.). Hecate: Deities & Demons. JSouthernStudio. https://www.jsouthernstudio.com/blogs/esotericinsights/hecate-goddess-of-the-month-october-2019

Kabir, S. R. (2023, January 12). Hel: Norse goddess of death and the underworld. History Cooperative; The History Cooperative. https://historycooperative.org/hel-norse-goddess-of-death/

Kabir, S. R. (2023, March 20). The Morrigan: Celtic goddess of war and fate. History Cooperative; The History Cooperative. https://historycooperative.org/morrigan/

Keys, K. H. (n.d.-a). Hekate and the Moon: History and Rituals. Keeping Her Keys. https://keepingherkeys.com/blog/f/hekate-and-the-moon-history-and-rituals

Keys, K. H. (n.d.-b). Hekate's Colors, Numbers, Stones And Symbols. Keeping Her Keys. https://keepingherkeys.com/f/hekates-colors-numbers-stones-and-symbols

Khamesra, M. (2021, October 23). Goddess Chamunda Devi (Matrika). Manish Jaishree; Jaishree Khamesra. https://manishjaishree.com/chamunda/

Kolton, M. (2023, August 23). Working with the Dark Goddess: A Journey Through the Dark Night of the Soul. Medium. https://alchemicalwombgoddess.medium.com/working-with-the-dark-goddess-a-journey-through-the-dark-night-of-the-soul-8bcbfe3d506e

Kyteler, E. (2023, August 4). Hekate's Sacred Animals: Symbolic Meanings of Dogs, Crows, and Snakes - Eclectic Witchcraft. Eclectic Witchcraft. https://eclecticwitchcraft.com/hekates-sacred-animals/

Landious Travel. (2022, April 9). Goddess Sekhmet - Iconography and Symbolism - Landious Travel. https://landioustravel.com/egypt/egyptian-deities/goddess-sekhmet/

Lee, K. A. (2022, April 6). 13 Formidable Examples of the Dark Goddess for 2023. The Moon School. https://www.themoonschool.org/divine-feminine/moon-goddess-series/what-is-the-dark-goddess-plus-13/

Lilith Archetype - 10 benefits of the "dark feminine" model. (2022, September 24). Santuário Lunar (Moon Shrine). https://www.santuariolunar.com/lilith-archetype/

Lilith. (n.d.). Fmarion.Edu. https://people.fmarion.edu/llarsen/LilithExplained.htm

Lockett, R. (2023, March 1). Cailleach: The Celtic goddess of winter. History Cooperative; The History Cooperative. https://historycooperative.org/cailleach/

López, J. S. (2021, October 26). Yewa - Yoruba Goddess of virginity and death. Symbol Sage. https://symbolsage.com/yewa-goddess-of-death/

Luna, B. (2016, August 22). Deep healing with A dark mother: Working with tantric goddess Chamunda —. The Hoodwitch. https://www.thehoodwitch.com/blog/2016/8/22/deep-healing-with-a-dark-mother-chamunda

Macha mythology project ms.Mc Cormac 6th class. (2022, November 23). Ennis National School. https://www.ennisns.ie/class-life-post/macha-mythology-project-ms-mc-cormack-6th-class/

Macha. (n.d.). Brooklynmuseum.org. https://www.brooklynmuseum.org/eascfa/dinner_party/heritage_floor/macha

Mackay, D. (2021, June 27). Everything you need to know about Hecate (maiden, mother, crone). TheCollector. https://www.thecollector.com/hecate-goddess-magic-witchcraft/

Mark, J. J. (2009). Hathor. World History Encyclopedia. https://www.worldhistory.org/Hathor/

Mark, J. J. (2010). Inanna. World History Encyclopedia. https://www.worldhistory.org/Inanna/

Mark, J. J. (2016). Nephthys. World History Encyclopedia. https://www.worldhistory.org/Nephthys/

Mark, J. J. (2017a). Ereshkigal. World History Encyclopedia. https://www.worldhistory.org/Ereshkigal/

Mark, J. J. (2019). Field of Reeds (aaru). World History Encyclopedia. https://www.worldhistory.org/Field_of_Reeds/

Mark, J. J. (2021). Hel. World History Encyclopedia. https://www.worldhistory.org/Hel/

Mark, J. J. (2021). Orisha. World History Encyclopedia. https://www.worldhistory.org/Orisha/

Mark, J. J. (2022). Inanna. World History Encyclopedia. https://www.worldhistory.org/Inanna/

Mark, J. J. (2023). Baba Yaga. World History Encyclopedia. https://www.worldhistory.org/Baba_Yaga/

Medium. (n.d.). Medium. https://medium.com/@judithshaw20/the-dark-goddess-empowers-consciousness-shifts-part-2-10fef83b0ba8

Meet the Dark Goddesses. (n.d.). The College of Psychic Studies. https://www.collegeofpsychicstudies.co.uk/enlighten/meet-the-dark-goddesses/

Meeting Hekate at Her Crossroads - Guided Meditation. (n.d.). SoundCloud. https://soundcloud.com/thewitchespath/meeting-hekate-at-her-crossroads-guided-meditation

Miate, L. (2022). Nyx. World History Encyclopedia. https://www.worldhistory.org/Nyx/

Mooney, S. (2020, June 20). The goddess Macha. Tales From The Wood. https://talesfromthewood.ie/the-goddess-macha-warrior-mother-and-queen/

Morana (Marzanna, Marena). (n.d.). Aminoapps. https://aminoapps.com/c/pagans-witches/page/item/morana-marzanna-marena/MQdW_bnET0I2kjkb1Lwm1mQN7nnZYPw3e4e

Morrigan, J. (2018, June 20). Litha Ritual for Nephthys. Pagan Muses. https://paganmuses.com/2018/06/21/litha-nephthys/

Morrigan. (n.d.). Mythopedia. https://mythopedia.com/topics/morrigan

Mythology, C. T. C. (2019, September 22). Sekhmet. Constructed Mythology. https://conmyth.fandom.com/wiki/Sekhmet

Nair, N. (2023, July 16). Unveiling the dark side: Evil Greek goddesses in mythology. Mythlok. https://mythlok.com/evil-greek-goddesses/

Nephthys | Egyptian Goddess of Death, Mythology & Symbolism | Study.com. (n.d.). study.com. https://study.com/academy/lesson/nephthys-facts-mythology-egyptian-goddess-death.html

Nephthys. (n.d.). https://occult-world.com/nephthys/

Nephthys. (n.d.). Mythopedia. https://mythopedia.com/topics/nephthys

New York Latin Culture Magazine. (2023, August 11). Yewá dances in the cemetery to help the dead move on. New York Latin Culture Magazine®.

https://www.newyorklatinculture.com/yewa-dances-in-the-cemetery-to-help-the-dead-move-on/

Noble, B. (2021, June 18). Marzanna/Morana - Slavic Goddess of Winter, Pestilence, and Death - Slavic Mythology Saturday - Brendan Noble. Brendan Noble. https://brendan-noble.com/marzanna-morana-goddess-of-winter-pestilence-and-death/

NORSE GODS: HEL - Ýdalir. (n.d.). Ydalir.Ca. https://ydalir.ca/norsegods/hel/

Norse mythology for Smart People - the ultimate online guide to Norse mythology and religion. (2012, November 14). Norse Mythology for Smart People. https://norse-mythology.org/

Nut - explore deities of ancient Egypt. (n.d.). Egyptianmuseum.org. https://egyptianmuseum.org/deities-nut

Nut -. (n.d.). Mythopedia. https://mythopedia.com/topics/nut

Nyx - Mythopedia. (n.d.). Mythopedia. https://mythopedia.com/topics/nyx

O'Connor, D. (2023, May 15). Cailleach - Irish goddess of the winter & her trail in Ireland. Irishcentral.com. https://www.irishcentral.com/travel/best-of-ireland/cailleach-irish-goddess-winter-trail-ireland

O'Hara, K. (2023, June 29). The Morrigan: The story of the fiercest goddess in Irish myth. The Irish Road Trip. https://www.theirishroadtrip.com/the-morrigan/

Oakes, H. (2019, April 9). Chinnamasta: The archetypal figure of the unconscious — Hayley Oakes, LM CPM. Hayley Oakes, LM CPM. https://www.hayleyoakes.com/articles/chinnamasta-the-archetypal-figure-of-the-unconscious

Ojukutu-Macauley, L. (2021, March 8). Women's International Day – West African earth goddess. Imọlẹ Candles. https://imolecandles.co.uk/blogs/news-1/women-s-international-day-west-african-earth-goddess

OldWorldGods. (2023, October 20). Celtic goddess Badb: Unveiling the mysterious power of the Battle Crow. Old World Gods. https://oldworldgods.com/celtics/celtic-goddess-badb/

Oliver, C. (2022, April 7). Angrboda. Vikings of Valhalla US. https://vikings-valhalla.com/blogs/norse-mythology/angrboda-norse-mythology

Onlinepuja. (n.d.). Steps to worship Goddess Durga. Onlinepuja.com. https://www.onlinepuja.com/blog/steps-worship-goddess-durga

Original Products. (2023, March 1). Orisha Oya: Ruler of storms and the wind. Original Botanica; www.originalbotanica.com#creator. https://originalbotanica.com/blog/orishas-oya-santeria

Oya, great goddess of the Wind. (n.d.). African American Wiccan Society. https://www.aawiccan.org/oya

Parikh, A. (2023, March 13). Sekhmet: Egypt's forgotten esoteric goddess. History Cooperative; The History Cooperative. https://historycooperative.org/sekhmet/

Pascale, S. (2020, September 16). The divine feminine. The Light Collective | Yoga Studio & Training - by Sian Pascale. https://www.thelightcollective.yoga/journal/durgamaa

Pchr, R. (2023, July 23). Chamunda: Unraveling the divine enigma. Braj Vrindavan Yatra. https://brajvrindavanyatra.com/2023/07/23/chamunda-unraveling-the-divine-enigma/

PERSEPHONE. (n.d.). Theoi.com. https://www.theoi.com/Khthonios/Persephone.html

Porteus, S. (2021, April 9). Baba Yaga — Creative Countryside. Creative Countryside. https://www.creativecountryside.com/blog/baba-yaga

Rajhans, S. G. (2007, October 15). The goddess Durga: The mother of the Hindu universe. Learn Religions. https://www.learnreligions.com/goddess-durga-1770363

Ramesh. (2019, September 1). Chinnamasta - the headless tantric goddess of transformation. VedicFeed. https://vedicfeed.com/chinnamasta-goddess-of-transformation/

Rhys, D. (2020, November 27). Badb - the Celtic goddess of war. Symbol Sage. https://symbolsage.com/badb-celtic-war-goddess/

Rhys, D. (2020, October 20). Skadi – Norse goddess of mountains and hunting. Symbol Sage. https://symbolsage.com/skadi-norse-goddess-hunting/

Rhys, D. (2021, January 7). Goddess Kali: The Hindu mother, warrior, and protector. Symbol Sage. https://symbolsage.com/kali-goddess-of-hinduism/

Rhys, D. (2022, April 18). Oya – the African goddess of weather. Symbol Sage. https://symbolsage.com/oya-goddess-of-weather/

Rhys, D. (2023, April 26). Nephthys - goddess of darkness and death in Egyptian mythology. Symbol Sage. https://symbolsage.com/nephthys-goddess-of-darkness-egyptian/

Rhys, D. (2023, February 7). The deep symbolism and powers of goddess Durga (Hinduism). Symbol Sage. https://symbolsage.com/durga-goddess-of-hinduism/

Richard. (2023, January 1). Who is Angrboda in Norse Mythology? The Giantess Grief-Bringer. Mythologyplanet.com. https://mythologyplanet.com/angrboda-norse-mythology-grief-bringer/

Rokvity, A. (2019, September 30). Goddess Durga: The embodiment of pure force. Yogapedia.com; Goddess Durga: The Embodiment of Pure Force. https://www.yogapedia.com/goddess-durga-the-embodiment-of-pure-force/2/11758

Scarletarosa. (2019, September 6). Ereshkigal. Tumblr. https://scarletarosa.tumblr.com/post/187530004051/ereshkigalmesopotamian-goddess-of-death-queen-of

Sekhmet. (n.d.). Egyptianmuseum.org. https://egyptianmuseum.org/deities-sekhmet

Sever, A. (2023, February 17). Hathor, the Goddess of Love: Powers, Rituals, Prayers, Offerings. Occultist. https://occultist.net/goddess-hathor-ritual-prayers-powers/

Shabnamdeep. (2023, September 13). The origins and myths of Goddess Durga. Goddess Gift. https://goddessgift.com/goddesses/durga/

SHADES OF A GODDESS - By Johnny Guthrie - Google Arts & Culture. (n.d.). Google Arts & Culture. https://artsandculture.google.com/usergallery/SgIS2pLQrfZaIQ

Sharma, M. (2023, October 17). Navratri 2023: How to worship Goddess Durga during Navaratri festival. Times Of India. https://timesofindia.indiatimes.com/religion/festivals/navratri-2023-how-to-worship-goddess-durga-during-navaratri-festival/articleshow/104494008.cms

Shaw, J. (2023, July 26). The Dark Goddess Empowers Consciousness Shifts, Part 1. Medium. https://medium.com/@judithshaw20/the-dark-goddess-empowers-consciousness-shifts-part-1-20ac63df5a63

Sir, P. (2021, October 24). Skadi Norse goddess facts and symbols meaning. Pirate Jewelry. https://piratejewellery.com/norse-mythology/skadi-norse-goddess-facts-and-symbols-meaning/

Skadi – the giantess who married the sea god. (n.d.). Historiska.Se. https://historiska.se/norse-mythology/skadi-en/

Skadi (mythology). (n.d.). Heroes Wiki; Fandom, Inc. https://hero.fandom.com/wiki/Skadi_(mythology)

Skadi goddess of winter. (2021, March 26). The Danish Canadian. https://www.danishcanadianmuseum.com/post/skadi-goddess-of-winter

Skadi. (2012, November 15). Norse Mythology for Smart People. https://norse-mythology.org/gods-and-creatures/giants/skadi/

Skadi. (n.d.). Newworldencyclopedia.org. https://www.newworldencyclopedia.org/entry/Skadi

Skjalden. (2020a, August 11). Angrboda. Nordic Culture. https://skjalden.com/angrboda/

Skjalden. (2020b, August 27). Hel is NOT the Norse Goddess of Death - Norse Mythology. Nordic Culture. https://skjalden.com/hel/

Slavs, M. T., & Slavs, M. T. (2022, May 14). Marzanna or Morana: Slavic Goddess of Death. Meet the Slavs. https://meettheslavs.com/marzanna-or-morana/

Smith, M. (2023, September 10). Badb. Goddess Gift; The Goddess Path. https://goddessgift.com/goddesses/badb/

Stanic, Z. (2023, April 7). Oya – Santeria goddess of storm, lightning, and death. Goddess Gift; The Goddess Path. https://goddessgift.com/goddesses/oya/

Stanic, Z. (2023b, September 12). The Morrigan – Celtic goddess of death, war and transformation. Goddess Gift. https://goddessgift.com/goddesses/the-morrigan/

Stanic, Z. (2023c, September 12). Yewa – Santeria Goddess of death and virginity. Goddess Gift. https://goddessgift.com/goddesses/yewa/

Sullivan, K. (2016, November 26). The mythology of nut, mother of gods. Ancient Origins. https://www.ancient-origins.net/myths-legends/mythology-nut-mother-gods-007084

tea and rosemary. (2021, April 21). 8+ Incredible Dark Goddesses & How To Work With Them. Tea & Rosemary. https://teaandrosemary.com/dark-goddesses/

Terravara. (2022, December 22). Working with Sekhmet: Offerings, Herbs, Crystals & More. Terravara. https://www.terravara.com/working-with-sekhmet/

The Dark Goddess As Archetype. (2010, November 1). Rounwytha. https://rounwytha.wordpress.com/2010/11/01/the-dark-goddess-as-archetype/

The Dark Goddess: A Post-Jungian Interpretation. (2018, October 19). The Religious Studies Project. https://www.religiousstudiesproject.com/response/the-dark-goddess-a-post-jungian-interpretation/

The Editors of Encyclopaedia Britannica. (1998, July 20). Baba Yaga | Characteristics, Family, & Mischief. Encyclopedia Britannica. https://www.britannica.com/topic/Baba-Yaga

The Editors of Encyclopaedia Britannica. (1998, July 20). Ereshkigal | Underworld, Queen, Sumerian. Encyclopedia Britannica. https://www.britannica.com/topic/Ereshkigal

The Editors of Encyclopaedia Britannica. (2023a, September 8). Hathor | Mother Goddess, Sky Goddess, Cow Goddess. Encyclopedia Britannica. https://www.britannica.com/topic/Hathor-Egyptian-goddess

The Editors of Encyclopaedia Britannica. (2023b, September 25). Skadi | Goddess, Jotun, Hunting. Encyclopedia Britannica. https://www.britannica.com/topic/Skadi

The Editors of Encyclopaedia Britannica. (2023c, October 23). Nut | Sky, Moon & Stars. Encyclopedia Britannica. https://www.britannica.com/topic/Nut-Egyptian-goddess

The Editors of Encyclopedia Britannica. (2022). Ishtar. In Encyclopedia Britannica.

The Editors of Encyclopedia Britannica. (2022). Niflheim. In Encyclopedia Britannica.

The Editors of Encyclopedia Britannica. (2023). Skadi. In Encyclopedia Britannica.

The Sect of the Horned God. (2023, February 25). The Dark Goddess Archetype. The Sect of the Horned God. https://www.thesectofthehornedgod.com/?p=5624

Thebacchichuntress. (2015, August 20). Offerings to Nyx. Tumblr. https://thebacchichuntress.tumblr.com/post/127160005123/offerings-to-nyx

Tlredmond. (2017, December 6). Characteristics - Baba Yaga. https://diorite.roanoke.edu/students/Fall2017/INQ270G3/tlredmond/?p=94

Tolentino, C. (2023, February 3). Macha: War Goddess of Ancient Ireland | History Cooperative. History Cooperative. https://historycooperative.org/macha/

Tolentino, C. (2023, January 30). Macha: War goddess of ancient Ireland. History Cooperative; The History Cooperative. https://historycooperative.org/macha/

Took, T. (n.d.). Lilith, Sumerian Demon Goddess and First Wife of Adam. Thaliatook.Com. https://www.thaliatook.com/AMGG/lilith.php

Turnbull, L. (2023, April 7). Nut - Egyptian "mother of all gods." Goddess Gift; The Goddess Path. https://goddessgift.com/goddesses/nut/

Turnbull, L. (2023a, September 12). Inanna: Ancient Sumerian Goddess of Heaven. Goddess Gift. https://goddessgift.com/goddesses/inanna/

Turnbull, L. (2023b, September 12). Nut: Egyptian Goddess 'Mother of All Gods.' Goddess Gift. https://goddessgift.com/goddesses/nut/

Turnbull, L. (2023c, September 12). Persephone: Greek Goddess Of Innocence And Queen Of The Underworld. Goddess Gift. https://goddessgift.com/goddesses/persephone/

Twelfthremedy. (2020, April 11). Hecate offerings. Tumblr. https://twelfthremedy.tumblr.com/post/615056721068605440/hecate-offerings

Underworld gods & goddesses. (n.d.). Theoi.com. https://www.theoi.com/greek-mythology/underworld-gods.html

Victory, F. (n.d.). The mythical journey of Oya: An exploration of African mythology. Oriire.com. https://www.oriire.com/article/the-mythical-journey-of-oya-an-exploration-of-african-mythology

Villines, Z. (2022, August 30). What is shadow work? Benefits and exercises. Medicalnewstoday.com. https://www.medicalnewstoday.com/articles/what-is-shadow-work

White Moon Gallery - Sekhmet. (n.d.). https://orderwhitemoon.org/goddess/sekhmet/Sekhmet2.html

Who Is The Norse Equivalent Of Persephone? (2023, October 14). Viking Style. https://viking.style/who-is-the-norse-equivalent-of-persephone/

Wigington, P. (2019, September 17). Introduction to Slavic Mythology. ThoughtCo. https://www.thoughtco.com/slavic-mythology-4768524

Wiki, C. T. F. (n.d.). Baba Yaga. Fairytale Wiki. https://fairytale.fandom.com/wiki/Baba_Yaga

Willemain-Green, C. (2020, April 9). Inanna's Descent: How We Embrace the Shadow and Integrate Our Wholeness. Earth Daughters. https://www.earthdaughters.org/library/innana-goddess

Willemain-Green, C. (2020, March 22). Lilith the Original Woman: Reclaiming the Wild Instinctual Nature of Woman. Earth Daughters. https://www.earthdaughters.org/library/lilith-goddess

Witchery. (2008, February 11). Goddess Candle Colors. Witchery. https://witchery.wordpress.com/2008/02/11/goddess-candle-colors/

Yap, S. S. (2022, November 9). How to Use the Hecate's Wheel Symbol. Blessed Be Magick. https://blessedbemagick.com/blogs/news/how-to-use-the-hecates-wheel-symbol

Yewá: Orisha of purity and chastity in Santeria. (2021, October 18). Oshaeifa.com. https://en.oshaeifa.com/orisha/yewa/

Zhelyazkov, Y. (2023, June 29). Macha: Celtic goddess of power, fertility, and war. Symbol Sage. https://symbolsage.com/macha-irish-goddess/

Arain, N. (2017). Goddess Empowerment. Createspace Independent Publishing Platform.

Asavei, M. A., & Bushnell, A. M. (2022). Feminist spirituality and Roma artistic activism: the Afterlife of the uncanonised Saint Sara Kali. Identities, 1-18.

Begg, E. (2017). The Cult of the Black Virgin. Chiron Publications.

Belloni, A., & Fox, M. (2019). Healing journeys with the black madonna: chants, music, and sacred practices of the great goddess. Bear & Company.

Courtney Hall Lee. (2017). Black Madonna: a womanist look at Mary of Nazareth. Cascade Books, An Imprint Of Wipf And Stock Publishers.

Georgieff, S. (2016). The black madonna: mysterious soul companion / Stepanie Georgieff. Outskirts Press.

Grace, A. (2021). Divine Feminine Energy. Stonebank Publishing.

Gustafson, F. (2009). The Black Madonna of Einsiedeln. Daimon Verlag.

Małgorzata Oleszkiewicz-Peralba. (2007). The Black Madonna in Latin America and Europe.

Marsman, M. A. (2019). Kali: in praise of the goddess. Psychological perspectives.

Mato, T. (1994). The Black Madonna Within. Open Court Publishing.

Michello, J. (2020). The black madonna: A theoretical framework for the African origins of other world religious beliefs. Religions.

Price, I., & Judith, A. (2017). Goddess Power: Awakening the Wisdom of the Divine Feminine in Your Life. Mango Media.

Strand, C., & Lytle, W. (2022). Waking up to the dark: the Black Madonna's gospel for an age of extinction and collapse. Monkfish Book Publishing Company.

Stuckey, J. H. (2005). Ancient mother goddesses and fertility cults. Journal of the Motherhood Initiative for Research and Community Involvement

# Image Sources

[1] https://pixabay.com/photos/woman-angel-raven-dark-fashion-8171684/

[2] https://unsplash.com/photos/a-statue-of-a-man-and-a-woman-shaking-hands-TjPcQQxgvI8

[3] Zde, CC BY-SA 4.0 <https://creativecommons.org/licenses/by-sa/4.0>, via Wikimedia Commons: https://commons.wikimedia.org/wiki/File:Relief_triplicate_Hekate_marble,_Hadrian_clasicism,_Prague_Kinsky,_NM-H10_4742,_151724.jpg

[4] Wolfgang Sauber, CC BY-SA 3.0 <https://creativecommons.org/licenses/by-sa/3.0>, via Wikimedia Commons: https://commons.wikimedia.org/wiki/File:AMI_-_Isis-Persephone.jpg

[5] https://commons.wikimedia.org/wiki/File:BnF_MS_Gr139_folio_435_verso_-_detail_-_Nyx.jpg

[6] https://pixabay.com/photos/hieroglyphs-goddess-queen-pharaoh-67471/

[7] FDRMRZUSA, CC BY-SA 4.0 <https://creativecommons.org/licenses/by-sa/4.0>, via Wikimedia Commons: https://commons.wikimedia.org/wiki/File:Sekhmet_mirror.svg

[8] Jeff Dahl, CC BY-SA 4.0 <https://creativecommons.org/licenses/by-sa/4.0>, via Wikimedia Commons: https://commons.wikimedia.org/wiki/File:Nepthys.svg

[9] Jeff Dahl, CC BY-SA 4.0 <https://creativecommons.org/licenses/by-sa/4.0>, via Wikimedia Commons: https://commons.wikimedia.org/wiki/File:Hathor.svg

[10] Eternal Space, CC BY-SA 4.0 <https://creativecommons.org/licenses/by-sa/4.0>, via Wikimedia Commons: https://commons.wikimedia.org/wiki/File:Nut_(goddess).png

[11] https://commons.wikimedia.org/wiki/File:Lilith_Periodo_de_Isin_Larsa_y_Babilonia.JPG

[12] Sailko, CC BY 3.0 <https://creativecommons.org/licenses/by/3.0>, via Wikimedia Commons: https://commons.wikimedia.org/wiki/File:Ishtar_on_an_Akkadian_seal.jpg

[13] *Messir, CC BY-SA 4.0 <https://creativecommons.org/licenses/by-sa/4.0>, via Wikimedia Commons.* https://commons.wikimedia.org/wiki/File:Babajeaga.jpg

[14] https://commons.wikimedia.org/wiki/File:Bilibin._Baba_Yaga.jpg

[15] *Dušan Božić, CC BY-SA 3.0 <https://creativecommons.org/licenses/by-sa/3.0>, via Wikimedia Commons:* https://commons.wikimedia.org/wiki/File:Morana_by_Du%C5%A1an_Bo%C5%BEi%C1%87.jpg

[16] *Ms Sarah Welch, CC BY-SA 4.0 <https://creativecommons.org/licenses/by-sa/4.0>, via Wikimedia Commons.* https://commons.wikimedia.org/wiki/File:3_Shaktism_goddesses_Devi_collage.jpg

[17] https://commons.wikimedia.org/wiki/File:Kali_by_Raja_Ravi_Varma.jpg

[18] https://commons.wikimedia.org/wiki/File:Durga_Mahisasuramardini.JPG

[19] https://commons.wikimedia.org/wiki/File:Chinnamasta_above_Kama_and_Rati_on_a_lotus_flower_-_18th_century_Nepalese_painting.jpg

[20] https://commons.wikimedia.org/wiki/File:Chamunda_Dancing_-_1700.jpg

[21] *Hammed usman, CC BY-SA 4.0 <https://creativecommons.org/licenses/by-sa/4.0>, via Wikimedia Commons* https://commons.wikimedia.org/wiki/File:A_statue_signifying_the_maternity_nature_of_iya_osun_at_the_sacred_grove_of_oshun2-1.jpg

[22] *Stevengravel, CC BY-SA 3.0 <https://creativecommons.org/licenses/by-sa/3.0>, via Wikimedia Commons:* https://commons.wikimedia.org/wiki/File:Oya.jpg

[23] *Rosemania, CC BY 2.0 <https://creativecommons.org/licenses/by/2.0>, via Wikimedia Commons.* https://commons.wikimedia.org/wiki/File:Epona.jpg

[24] https://commons.wikimedia.org/wiki/File:Macha.jpg

[25] *Internet Archive Book Images, No restrictions, via Wikimedia Commons:* https://commons.wikimedia.org/wiki/File:Wonder_tales_from_Scottish_myth_and_legend_(1917)_(14566397697).jpg

[26] *Internet Archive Book Images, No restrictions, via Wikimedia Commons.* https://commons.wikimedia.org/wiki/File:Old_Norse_stories_(1900)_(14595035089).jpg

[27] https://commons.wikimedia.org/wiki/File:Hel_(the_personification_of_Hel).png

[28] https://commons.wikimedia.org/wiki/File:Skadi_Hunting_in_the_Mountains_by_H._L._M.jpg

[29] https://commons.wikimedia.org/wiki/File:Lokis_Gez%C3%BCcht.jpg

[30] *Internet Archive Book Images, No restrictions, via Wikimedia Commons.* https://commons.wikimedia.org/wiki/File:The_olive_fairy_book_(1907)_(14750441274).jpg

[31] *Rebecca Radcliff, CC BY-SA 2.0 <https://creativecommons.org/licenses/by-sa/2.0>, via Wikimedia Commons.* https://commons.wikimedia.org/wiki/File:The_Imbolc_Ritual_Altar.jpg

[32] https://commons.wikimedia.org/wiki/File:Gorczyn_Black_Madonna_of_Cz%C4%99stochowa.jpg

[33] *Csiraf, CC BY-SA 3.0 <https://creativecommons.org/licenses/by-sa/3.0>, via Wikimedia Commons:* https://commons.wikimedia.org/wiki/File:Black_Madonna.jpg

[34] https://www.pexels.com/photo/loving-mother-with-son-in-park-5268322/

[55] https://www.pexels.com/photo/2-person-holding-hands-45842/
[56] https://pixabay.com/illustrations/wisdom-power-vision-feeling-mind-666135/
[57] https://commons.wikimedia.org/wiki/File:Egyptian_-_Isis_with_Horus_the_Child_-_Walters_54416_-_Three_Quarter_Right.jpg
[58] shakko, CC BY-SA 3.0 <https://creativecommons.org/licenses/by-sa/3.0>, via Wikimedia Commons: https://commons.wikimedia.org/wiki/File:Ceres_(Pio-Clementino)_cast_in_Pushkin_museum.jpg
[59] Getty Villa, CC BY-SA 2.0 <https://creativecommons.org/licenses/by-sa/2.0>, via Wikimedia Commons: https://commons.wikimedia.org/wiki/File:Cybele_Getty_Villa_57.AA.19.jpg
[40] Commonists, CC BY-SA 4.0 <https://creativecommons.org/licenses/by-sa/4.0>, via Wikimedia Commons: https://commons.wikimedia.org/wiki/File:Diana_of_Versailles.jpg
[41] https://commons.wikimedia.org/wiki/File:Kali_lithograph.jpg
[42] https://pixabay.com/illustrations/meditation-spiritual-yoga-1384758/
[43] https://pixabay.com/illustrations/aware-awake-accepting-attuned-1353780/
[44] https://www.pexels.com/photo/woman-spreading-both-her-arms-2529375/
[45] https://pixabay.com/illustrations/board-writing-chalk-blackboard-953151/
[46] LatakiaHill, CC BY-SA 4.0 <https://creativecommons.org/licenses/by-sa/4.0>, via Wikimedia Commons: https://commons.wikimedia.org/wiki/File:Candlelight_Vigil_at_University_of_Chicago_for_Urumchi_Fire.jpg
[47] https://www.pexels.com/photo/silhouette-of-person-raising-its-hand-268134/
[48] SICDAMNOME, CC BY-SA 4.0 <https://creativecommons.org/licenses/by-sa/4.0>, via Wikimedia Commons: https://commons.wikimedia.org/wiki/File:Our_Lady_of_Consolation_Grinstead_Great_Britain.jpg
[49] Judgefloro, CC0, via Wikimedia Commons: https://commons.wikimedia.org/wiki/File:8456Marian_Healing_Exhibit_with_Saints_18.jpg
[50] Martin Dürrschnabel, CC BY-SA 2.5 <https://creativecommons.org/licenses/by-sa/2.5>, via Wikimedia Commons: https://commons.wikimedia.org/wiki/File:Schwarze_Madonna.jpg
[51] https://commons.wikimedia.org/wiki/File:1531_Nuestra_Se%C3%B1ora_de_Guadalupe_anagoria.jpg
[52] Virgendelosremedios, CC BY-SA 4.0 <https://creativecommons.org/licenses/by-sa/4.0>, via Wikimedia Commons: https://commons.wikimedia.org/wiki/File:Coronada_Juquila.jpg
[53] Flyer20061, CC BY-SA 3.0 <https://creativecommons.org/licenses/by-sa/3.0>, via Wikimedia Commons: https://commons.wikimedia.org/wiki/File:Our_Lady_of_Loreto.jpg
[54] S. Finner: Siddhartha Finner, Dipl.Ing.-Architektur, CC BY-SA 3.0 <https://creativecommons.org/licenses/by-sa/3.0>, via Wikimedia Commons: https://commons.wikimedia.org/wiki/File:Gnadenbild,_Gnadenkapelle_Alt%C3%B6tting.jpeg
[55] https://commons.wikimedia.org/wiki/File:Statue_Notre-Dame_de_La_Sarte.jpg
[56] See page for author, CC BY-SA 3.0 <http://creativecommons.org/licenses/by-sa/3.0/>, via

Wikimedia Commons: https://commons.wikimedia.org/wiki/File:Procession_2006_-_n%C2%B06.JPG

[57] https://commons.wikimedia.org/wiki/File:Black_virgin_of_russia.jpg

[58] No machine-readable author provided. Severus assumed (based on copyright claims). CC BY-SA 3.0 <http://creativecommons.org/licenses/by-sa/3.0/>, via Wikimedia Commons: https://commons.wikimedia.org/wiki/File:Marija_Bistrica.jpg

[59] Hyppolyte de Saint-Rambert, CC BY-SA 4.0 <https://creativecommons.org/licenses/by-sa/4.0>, via Wikimedia Commons: https://commons.wikimedia.org/wiki/File:Santiago_Virgen_de_La_Caridad_del_Cobre_hdsr_S5is_Cuba2_841.jpg

[60] https://commons.wikimedia.org/wiki/File:Municipal_Gallery_of_Ioannina_-_Mother_of_God_Eleousa_of_Kykkos_1860.jpg

www.ingramcontent.com/pod-product-compliance
Lightning Source LLC
Chambersburg PA
CBHW051855160426
43209CB00006B/1308